J.B. CROWLE.

For

Tom & Simon

BODMIN RIDING

Written, printed, bound & published in Bodmin,
County Town of Cornwall.

£1

BODMIN RIDING

The authoress & publishers express appreciation to

THE SADDLERY & LEATHER SHOP, BODMIN

for sponsoring this volume.

FIRST EDITION MAY 1975

Printed & Bound in Bodmin by duchy press *for Bodmin Books Ltd.*

BODMIN RIDING

&

OTHER SIMILAR CELTIC CUSTOMS

by

PAT MUNN, B.A.

authoress of BODMIN MOOR & THE CORNISH CAPITAL

With a foreword by IVOR WHITING, Freeman of Bodmin

Chief Executive Officer: North Cornwall District Council

Illustrations by J.B. Crowle.

BODMIN BOOKS LIMITED

Cornish County Town Publishers

45, Fore Street, Bodmin, Cornwall, PL31 2JA, United Kingdom

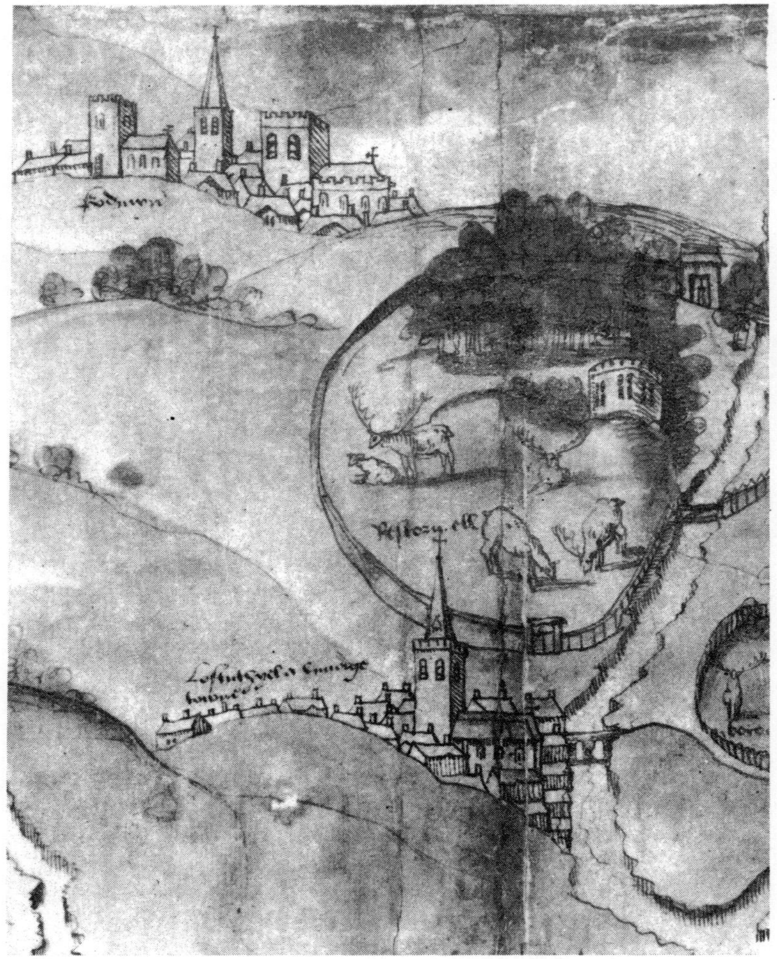

EARLY 16th CENTURY MAP OF BODMIN & LOSTWITHIEL, WHEN BOTH HAD 'RIDINGS'.

Top left: Bodmin's spired parish church, c.40 years after rebuilding, between the friary (left) & priory (right) churches. See page 11.

Foreground: Lostwithiel, in the Fowey valley, below the Duke of Cornwall's Restormel Castle & deer park. See page 82.

(British Library Dept. of Manuscripts. Cotton Ms Augustus I; 38; reproduced by permission of the British Library Board).

BODMIN RIDING

CONTENTS

ACKNOWLEDGMENTS

my appreciation is extended to

MR. IVOR WHITING for his foreword and for reading a proof of the work.

MR. L.E. LONG, Bodmin Museum Curator, for checking a typescript and supplying some of the press references, tunes and old photographs.

BODMIN TOWN COUNCIL for access to its museum & permission to use archive materials.

BODMIN LIBRARY STAFF for assistance during research.

MRS. C. NORTH, Senior Assistant Archivist: Cornwall Record Office, for help with manuscript evidence; and the County Archivist for permission to quote.

MR. C.R. CLEMENS for permission to publish photographs acknowledged as his; and for rendering my efforts worthy of joining them in this work.

MR. F.E. HALLIDAY for permission to include extracts from his edition of Carew's 'Survey'.

MR. W.H. PAYNTER for permission to include the extract from his edition of Allen's 'Liskeard'.

MR. W.G. HARRIS, Assistant Keeper: Bodleian Library Western Manuscripts Department, for locating the Lhuyd extract; & the Keeper for permission to quote.

MR. M.A.F. BORRIE, Assistant Keeper: British Library Manuscripts Department for locating the W.R.Gilbert extract; & the Keeper for permission to quote.

MR. D. FOWLER, London Express News & Feature Services, for locating the Sunday Express extract; and the Editor for permission to quote.

MR. J.D. ARMSTRONG, Senior Information Librarian: Cornwall Library, for locating the Cox and Heath extracts; & the County Librarian for permission to quote.

MR. H.L. DOUCH, Royal Institution Of Cornwall Curator, as custodian of the 19th century newspapers, R.I.C. journal and Henderson manuscripts quoted.

MR. C.W. WICKS, Editor: Cornish Guardian, for permission to include extracts from his newspaper.

MR. A.K. HAMILTON JENKIN, for permission to cite examples from his works

AND THE FOLLOWING WHO HAVE assisted by lending photographs and books, answering queries and by helping in other ways:
Mr. D. Hore; Mr. & Mrs. D. Hamilton; the Rev. A.S.W. Barrie, Vicar of Bodmin; Commander W.R.Gilbert of Compton Castle; Mrs. M. Larsen; Mr. & Mrs. J.C.G. Parkin; Mrs. M. Perry; Mr. & Mrs. J.H. and Miss K. Pethybridge; Mrs. E.M. Bound.

Photographs in this book, with the exceptions of those dated 1923 and 1930, are of the 1974 Riding; design and illustrations are by the authoress unless otherwise stated.

It is hoped that readers will agree with the decision to exclude a Bibliography in favour of giving the locations of manuscripts, rare books and old newspapers where extracts from them are reviewed in this volume. Reference works by such as Maclean, Polwhele, the brothers Lysons, C.S.Gilbert, Drew, Redding and Daniell may be consulted in the Cornish sections of most libraries or - with the journals and Leland's work - at the Royal Institution of Cornwall Museum at Truro. Other mentioned publications are available at retail stores; and Gross's 'Guild Merchant' may be obtained upon application to a library.

FOREWARD

Conservation is the concern and desire of many people in this day and age - and, I must confess, I am often tempted to ask why this desire appears to be directed mainly towards the physical. Are not the ancient customs and traditions of our country a reminder of our heritage and just as worthy as, say, some buildings of architectural interest or an ancient monument? However, to unearth the background of some traditions and customs is just as difficult as to undertake an archaeological 'dig', perhaps even more so, and often just as big a mystery.

Pat Munn has 'dug' very deeply indeed - this work covers conjecture of would-be interpreters over the past two hundred years and records spanning six centuries altogether.

Here, then, is a **different** historical 'who-dunit' or a 'who-did-what-and-why?' of a traditional celebration which was, and I hope will be again, a happy mixture of the religious and the secular, a custom honoured by the involvement of royalty. As the authoress says in her introduction, *'few can agree as to what the Riding is or was all about'* and herein lies the challenge of this book. Will you agree with **her** conclusions?

One thing seems certain - and that is that the Bodmin Riding was an important Cornish celebration.

The revival in 1974 started modestly, but my personal hope is that interest in it will grow so that it becomes again a permanent part of the calendar of Cornish customs. This book will give added interest to the Riding as well as be of help to all of those who want to know more about our traditions.

Ivor Whiting.

INTRODUCTION

Bodmin, although county town of Cornwall, name-town of a parliamentary division and administrative centre of the county's largest district, is essentially and traditionally a market place on the edge of the vast moorland to which is also lends name. Over the centuries, it has been noted for its horse fairs, its horse races and more recent shows, and for its mounted bounds-beating ceremony. Indeed, it has been said that the town's preoccupation with the horse-drawn omnibus in the last century lost it a place on the main-line railway; certainly the rivalry between the two principal omnibuses was such that, when members of the council took sides, they were known by their names - Town Arms and Royal!

Be that as it may, it is only to be expected that a town with such a long and close association with the horse and which has seen the splendour of a judge's arrival in his coach-and-six, should have as its annual festival a custom called the Riding. So much has been written about this event that it might be wondered why a book is necessary. In reality, however, no work of this length has ever been attempted on the subject for, it seems, few can agree as to what the Riding is or was all about. Such dispute has arisen mainly because as many records as may exist of the Riding have not been located, deciphered, analysed and compared in a single volume so that some conclusions can be reached as to its origin and meaning.

In attempting so ambitious a project, one would be foolhardy to imagine that a mystery, which has baffled would-be interpreters for close on two centuries, could as easily be solved. The Riding was old by the date of its first known record in 1469 and certain parts of it must for ever remain within the confines of enigma. Nevertheless, you are now invited to turn detective and to examine the evidence as presented in the various forms of accounts, letters, press reports and recollections and which, for the first time, is printed in one book.

six centuries' records of bodmin riding

1469-1472

BODMIN PARISH CHURCH REBUILDING ACCOUNTS
(Cornwall Record Office, Truro: B/BOD 244) -

1) *Memorandum that Thomas aforesaid has received of the*
   stewards of the Riding Guilds as for holding of . . . . . by . . .
   of ston made and ratid:

First for St. Loy's Guild of John Hancock·· · ·		*13.4d.*
Item of St. Petroc's Guild of Richard Colom · ·		*13.4d.*
Item of St. John's Guild of John Prout · ·		*£1.06.8d.*
Item of St. Anyan's Guild of Thomas Hay · ·		*£1.06.8d.*
Item of St. Martin's Guild of Thomas Fyk · ·		*13.4d.*
total · · · ·		*£4.13.4d.*

2) *Item of the Riding Guild, viz. of St. Loy's*
   Guild, eleventh year of Edward I V · · · ·   *10.0d.*

3) *Item at radar day · · · · · · · · · · · ·*   *11.0d.*

4) *Item received from the Riding Guild . . . . .*
   presented by the society from the Jantacle
   for this and the ensuing year · · · · · ·   *£9.06.8d.*

NOTES

*The four entries above are in order of their appearance on the original
and very long handwritten account of receipts and expenses; but they
are neither consecutive nor numbered in it. (See the third note under
the date 1814).

*Entry one above appears amongst receipts for 1469, 1470, up to Mich-
aelmas 1471 when Thomas Jerman was receiver. The Riding Guilds

would appear to have been five trades guilds for, with the exception of St. John's which was probably for drapers and tailors, we learn elsewhere in the accounts that St. Loy's which donated about 66½p above was for smiths, St. Petroc's was for skinners and glovers, St. Anyan's which donated about £1.33p was for shoemakers, and St. Martin's was for millers. The names connected with the guilds above change as the years alter in the accounts, presumably upon the elections of new stewards.

*While entry two above shows St. Loy's as *the* Riding Guild, giving 50p in 1471, although the other trades guilds appear in the same list, all are calling Riding Guilds in a later summary of this section.

*Entry 3 above occurs amongst expenses for 1469 and 1470 and seems to show that the receiver paid 55p on Riding Day.

*Entry 4 above shows that some proceeds of the Riding were donated towards the church rebuilding fund, the word *'Jantacle'* being used for 'the Riding and sports'; it may be noticed that the amount *'for this and the ensuing year'*, £9.33p, is twice the total of £4.66½p in entry one above which seems to show that the Riding Guilds had put aside a certain amount per year for the fund.

*Thomas Lucombe, then mayor, was the receiver for the final year of the appeal when receipts totalled £65.7.0d. and expenses £74.14.3d. Expenses for the previous years, when Jerman was receiver, were £194.3.6½d.; and receipts amounted to £196.7.4½d. of which the guilds contributed £86.11.5d. from their funds, £24.13.0d. from town collections and £4.13.4d. worth of wax. It may be seen from this that the guilds - some 40 of which are named in the accounts, including the Riding societies - did much to raise money and materials for the rebuilding project.

*According to Maclean's 'History of Bodmin', 1870, page 127 footnote *"the Riding Guild is mentioned in connection with the erection of Berry Tower"*. The 1501-14 parchment roll of accounts concerning this project is awaiting repair in the Cornwall Record Office: B/BOD 314. (Maclean's 'History of Bodmin' is also found in volume one of his 3-volume 'History Of The Deanery Of Trigg Minor', the above-mentioned reference being on page 227 of that work).

*Transcript of the church accounts: edited by J.J. Wilkinson, 1874, in the Camden Miscellany, volume VII, 1875; copies - Cornwall Record Office: DDEN 1907; or Truro and Bodmin libraries.

1583

AN ORDER TAKEN FOR SHOEMAKERS, BY THE MAYOR AND MASTERS OF THE OCCUPATION, NOV. 15
(Cornwall Record Office, Truro: B/BOD 243)

1. *No journeyman's wages to be above 2.0d.*
2. *A meaner workman to receive no more than he and his master agree.*
3. *On pain of 10.0d., a master not to employ a journeyman unless he left his last master with goodwill.*
4. *Taverners, permitting journeymen credit above 12d. will lose the surplus amount.*
5. *Any refusing to appear before the mayor or masters when summoned, to be fined 12d. for each offence and imprisoned until the debt is paid.*
6. *On pain of 3.4d., masters' stands at street fairs and markets to be in order of age, the eldest in the lowest positions and the youngest upwards.*
7. *"Item: more, that at the Riding, every master and journeyman shall give their attendance to the steward, and likewise to bring him to the church, upon pain of 12d. for every master and 6d. for a journeyman, for every such default, to the discretion of the masters of the occupation."*
8. *Anyone imprisoned by order of the masters to pay the bailiff's fee of 4d.*
9. *What every master shall pay by the week . . . . (some 15 entries such as 'John Evans, senior, Id')*

"Signed by me, Thomas Andro, mayor" (and others, presumably the masters)

NOTES

*Although in order of their appearance on the original manuscript, the nine entries above have been numbered for reference purposes and, with the exception of entry 7, they are paraphrased here.

*A 'journeyman', in entry 1 above, would have been a craftsman who, having served an appropriate apprenticeship, was qualified to ply his trade for wages which, in this case, were not more than 10p.

*A 'meaner workman', in entry 2 above, would have been an apprentice who was learning his craft and therefore legally bound to a master for an agreed period and keep.

*A 'master', in entry 3 above, was a craftsman of approved skill who employed others. In this order, he faced a fine of 50p if he employed a journeyman out of favour with the former employer.

*Entry 4 above shows that this guild could protect its skilled members from being sued for debt over a specified sum, in this case 5p, by outsiders.

*Entry 5 above illustrates the way in which the guild court had power to summon members before it, to fine them 5p for each refusal to appear and to imprison them until the debt was paid; those so impounded were required, by entry 8 above, to pay the officer's fee of about 1½p. Fines and fees, in this entry and in entries 3, 5, 6 and 7, seem heavy when compared with a skilled craftsman's wages in entry 1 above.

*Entry 6 above shows the strict order of precedence, enforced by a fine of 16½p, in this guild.

*Entry 7 above obliged skilled members of the guild to attend church during the Riding unless masters paid a 5p fine and journeymen 2½p; reference to the appendix concerning the Helston Shoemakers' Guild may explain the reason for enforced attendance.   (Page 96).

*In the parish church rebuilding accounts, we noticed that St. Anyan's Guild for shoemakers was described as a Riding Guild. In the order above, members of that guild are still apparently connected with the festival a century later.

*Transcript of the document: Bodmin Register, compiled by John Wallis, 1827-38, page 322; in the Cornwall Library or Record Office at Truro.

1602

RICHARD CAREW, 'Survey of Cornwall', two books, 1602; book two, Trigg Hundred -

"The youthlier sort of Bodmin townsmen use sometimes to sport themselves, by playing the box with strangers, whom they summon to Halgavor. The name signifies Goat's Moor, and such a place it is, lying a little without the town and very full of quagmires. When these mates meet with any raw servingman, or other young master, who may serve and deserve to make pastime, they cause him to be solemnly arrested for his appearance before the mayor of Halgavor, where he is charged with wearing one spur, or going untrussed or wanting a girdle, or some such like felony; and after he has been arraigned and tried, with all requisite circumstances, judgement is given in formal terms, and executed in some one ungracious prank or other, more to the scorn than hurt of the party condemned. Hence is sprung the proverb, when we see one slovenly apparelled, 'he shall be presented in Halgavor Court'. But now and then they extend this merriment with the largest, to the prejudice of over credulous people, persuading them to fight with a dragon lurking in Halgavor, or to see some strange matter there; which concludes at last with a training them into the mire."

NOTES

*Richard Carew, of Antony on the Lynher estuary, was known to have been working on his 'Survey' from about 1584 until its appearance in print when he was 46 years of age. The passage above was preceded by descriptions of Bodmin, the 1497 and 1549 rebellions, and a local schoolboys' prank; it was followed by a paragraph on Scarlet's Well.

*Although the writer was not particularly conversant with the Cornish language, he correctly translated Halgavor as Goats Moor if it derives from 'hal' and 'gever'; it may, however, derive from 'gover' and mean Stream Tinworking. But Carew's choice enabled him at once to adhere to contemporary literary fashion and play upon the word goat and thus to colour our reading of the passage.

*The place-name Dragon Pit still exists at Halgavor and is of interest on two accounts. Medieval church-goers would have been familiar with one of the lessons in the Life of 6th century St. Petroc; this featured a dragon who lived on a moor near the Saint's cell, allegorical of evil challenging his mission in the Bodmin area. And, when garlands were carried on the mounted beating of the bounds at Rogationtide, it was customary to parade an effigy of a dragon representing the devil which eventually met an ignominious end at a place thereafter called Dragon Pit, according to Dr. Couch.

*In his 1864 article in the Royal Institution of Cornwall journal, Dr. Couch wrote of the passage above: *"I know of no author besides Carew who makes independent mention of Halgavor Sports; and it would seem that Halgavor was the scene of perennial jokes; nor is it anywhere said that its usages and immunities were confined to any season. The Bodmin Riding is evidently quite distinct; though probably, at a time of great merry-making in the neighbourhood of the Moor, the 'ungracious pranks' may have been more than usually rife. No remembrance of Halgavor* **Court** *exists among people now resident in the neighbourhood."*

However - it will be seen that Cox and Heath described Halgavor sports without mentioning the Riding, that Polwhele and Drew dealt with each event separately and that Daniell's 1906 'Compendium' reported an observance of the court as lately as 1904. Moreover Cyrus Redding made *'independent mention'* of the sports in 1842; and appendices at the end of this book show that a mock court was part of Liskeard Riding and other similar festivities.

*Descriptions of the Riding in 1824 prove it to have been a festival of several parts, only some of which appealed to a particular reporter. Carew was a magistrate and therefore interested in court procedure, as the passage above confirms. But Bodmin was by no means the only place to have a mock official, nor is there much reason to believe that Halgavor Court was originally held at random or in isolation - reference to the appendices may suggest the reverse to be true. We may only speculate upon Halgavor Court's origin however. It could have been a burlesque of a guild or borough court; or it might have survived from the time when the Merchant Guild had power under a 13th century charter of Richard, Earl of Cornwall, to grant Bodmin's liberty to runaway serfs who had taken refuge in the borough and kept its peace 'for a year and a day'. The latter possibility would account for the proverb quoted by Carew for, presumably, even in medieval times such refugees may have been noticeable for their comparatively poor appearance and obviously awaiting presentation. One theory which has been put forward in connection with mock mayors is that the elections of such survive from the choosing of tribal chieftains: and that conquerors, such as the Saxons, tolerated these symbols of former independence during festivals.

*Modern edition of the passage above: "Richard Carew of Antony", edited by F.E. Halliday; Adams & Dart, 1969; page 197.

BODMIN RIDING

1691

AN ACCOUNT OF THE DISBURSEMENTS OF THOMAS MAY, MAYOR OF BODMIN, FROM SEP. 24 1690 TO SEP. 24 1691 (Cornwall Record Office, Truro: B/BOD 288; pages 3 & 4) -

1) *To the poor on Good Friday* .. .. .. £1.04.0d.

(8 entries between those above & below)

2) *Lady Day payment* .. .. £1.16.0d.

3) *The 26th April in wine on the justices at an adjourned sessions* .. .. 8.3d.

4) *Rogation week payment* .. .. 1.0d.

(10 entries between those above & below)

5) *Midsummer payment* .. .. £1.16.0d.

6) *For 4 bottles of wine presented to Mr. Robartes and other gentlemen at the Riding* .. .. 8.0d.

7) *Paid Thomas Hoskin for boar at the bonfire when Athlone was taken at the King's ringing day* .. .. 13.4d.

(3 entries between those above & below)

8) *Michaelmas payment* .. .. £1.16.0d.

NOTES

*With the exception of entries 1, 3, 6 and 7, those above are paraphrased here but they are all in order of their appearance on the original manuscript although some are not consecutive and none is numbered in it.

*September 24, in the manuscript's title, was the date of the Bodmin mayor-choosing under the borough charter then in force. The entries above therefore obviously refer to the year 1691; and, although our main interest is in entry 6, the others are shown here in order that we may attempt to date the latter.

*Maclean in his 'History of Bodmin', 1870, page 127 footnote mentioned *"1706-1707: 'a venison to the Riding from Mr. Robartes'."* This refers to mayoral accounts for that year when the office holder was, in fact, once again Thomas May. Mentioned as a councillor in the borough's 1685 charter, this mayor - whose burial is recorded for July 28, 1708 in the parish register - seems to have had the Riding at heart and might possibly have revived it after a lapse during the Commonwealth 1649-60. The 1706/7 mayoral entry also means that, taken with the 1690/1 entry above, we have detail beyond that afforded by Lhuyd's description in 1700.

*Lhuyd's account showed that some change had taken place in Riding procedure in that the church attendance had been discontinued by 1700; and the sports he described may be taken as having been held during May's mayoralties. Entry 6 above infers that some kind of banquet was held during the Riding, when Mayor May expended 40p to entertain Robartes of Lanhydrock House and other members of the gentry. Such an inference would find support in the 1706/7 mayoral accounts and W.R. Gilbert's comment in 1812; and further evidence of the gentry's patronage appears in the 1823 West Briton advertisement connected with the Bodmin Races which probably derived from the Riding sports. It now remains to discover an approximate date for the Riding in 1691 from the entries above,which appear to be the first hint as to the Riding's season.

*Good Friday, in entry 1 above when the mayor spent £1.20p, fell on April 10 in 1691. Lady Day, in entry 2 above when the mayor paid £1.80p (towards the ancient fee farm rent of £5.50p per year to the exchequer, in return for which the burgesses ordered their own affairs by leave of their royal charter) was March 25; other such quarter days when tenancies began and ended, employment was taken or given up and rents were due, were Midsummer June 24 in entry 5 above, Michaelmas September 29 in entry 8 above, and Christmas December 25. Entry 3 above is illustrative of the Quarter Sessions arrangements then in force whereby they began at Bodmin then adjourned to Truro for one quarter, and began at Truro then adjourned to Bodmin for the next; the latter procedure obtained at Easter 1691 when the mayor spent about 41p to entertain the J.P.s. Rogation week when the mayor expended 5p, in entry 4 above, followed the 5th Sunday after Easter and, as the latter fell on April 12 in 1691, the reference is to May 18-23. Finally, entry 7 above when the mayor spent 66½p refers to a celebration ordered by William III when the commander-in-chief of his Protestant army in Ireland, General Ginckel, took Athlone from the Roman Catholic supporters of the former king, James II, on June 30, 1691.

*From the position of entry 6 above, it seems that the Riding in 1691 took place at some time between Midsummer June 24 and the taking of Athlone on June 30, there being no specified date on the accounts. It is not possible to be sure, however, for at least two reasons: entry 1 above referring to April 10 is placed before entry 2 referring to March 25 suggesting that the mayor did not always enter items in strict date order; and, by the time the news of June 30 came through, the bonfire in entry 7 would probably have taken place in July so that the Riding could also have been in that month.

1700

NOTES ON BODMIN IN HANDWRITING SIMILAR IN SOME RESPECTS TO THAT OF EDWARD LHUYD
(Western Manuscripts Department, Bodleian Library, Oxford: Ms: Rawlinson D.997, folios 12 verso and 13 recto)

*"Their feast on the two Mondays right after St. Becket's day, at which time they have a great concourse of people that come a riding (as they call it) viz. they deck a piece of timber of about a man's height with various sorts of flowers and garlands and * carried it to church (formerly but not of late) and then to Bodmin downs they go all in body (all of a trade riding by themselves) to sports (for example) some ride for silver shoes (a piece of silver formed so) others run for silver rings etc.*
**first to church then afterwards to the downs, but of latter years they do not come to church at all with it but straight to the downs."*

NOTES

*Born in Cardiganshire in 1660, Lhuyd went to Oxford in 1682 and subsequently became keeper of the Ashmolean Museum. His work, collecting specimens and information for the foundation and various publications, took him all over the kingdom. The notes above, if they are as suspected his, would have been made during his tour of Cornwall towards the end of 1700. In a later passage, the writer mentions by name several Bodmin residents who had reached advanced years of age, two being over 100; and it is assumed that he was able to draw upon the long memories of such persons.

*The passage above seems to be the first to indicate an actual time for the Riding - two Mondays after Becket's Day. As the latter was the observance of the martyr's translation on July 7, the Riding in 1700 appears to have taken place in the month suggested by the 1691 mayoral accounts entry. It may be noted however that, although a chantry dedicated to Becket was erected in the churchyard during Edward III's reign, the guild connected with it is nowhere recorded as having had particular association with the Riding so that Bodmin's annual celebration is unlikely to have been in honour of the martyr. As we remark in the final note under the dates 1823, 1824, 1825, Lhuyd's mention of Becket's Day could have been incidental; but, in any case, he is known to have blundered regarding a patronal feast date (G.H. Doble, "Saints of Cornwall", book 5, page 5 footnote). Nevertheless, if the Riding was, as Lhuyd described it, a parish *"feast"* the Day of one of Bodmin's patrons - that of King Edgar on July 8

does coincide with Lhuyd's timing. (See under 1903; and Appendix 1)
*The writer gives us the first known record of a garlanded pole being
borne aloft during the Riding. The flowers of Midsummer were probably of significance originally and certainly link the Riding with other
folk customs, as we outline under the heading Comments & Conclusions.   (See page 78).

*As we have seen, the church was connected with the Riding in the
15th and 16th centuries; but, by the time the passage above was
compiled, something had happened which changed the procedural
pattern so that the church no longer featured. The occurrence that
immediately springs to mind is the lightning strike on the church in
December of 1699; but, as this took place only months before Lhuyd's
arrival and he expressly states that they did not come to church *"of
latter years"*, the upheaval of the Civil War seems more likely to have
caused the change. The old guilds had vanished by the time such
festivities were banned during the Commonwealth, 1649-1660, and
the church, once the centre of community life, had long lost that
position. It would therefore appear, from Lhuyd's account, that
Riding participants had attended church prior to their sports before
1649; but, when the custom was revived - perhaps at the Restoration,
or even by Mayor May as late as in 1691 - the sports were all important and the church attendance was not resumed. We may assume
however, that the Riding comprised much more than the events so
briefly noted by Lhuyd in 1700 as Mayor May's accounts, showing
wine and venison connected with the gentry, suggest that a banquet
was held at least in the years either side of Lhuyd's visit - 1691 and
1707. This would be in keeping with what is known of parish feasts
and town festivals as illustrated in the appendices.
*Obviously, from Lhuyd's description of *"all of a trade riding by
themselves"*, the old guilds order still obtained in the Riding procession. The site of the sports outlined in the passage above is, however,
difficult to locate with certainty. The name Bodmin Downs is how
applied to the Racecourse and area but, according to a map attached
to the Municipal Corporation Boundaries Commission Report of 1837,
land adjacent to the Beacon was so designated at that time. (See
third note under the date 1820).
*Lhuyd's description of sports is of great importance and interest.
Firstly, it confirms our suspicion that they were part of the Riding,
the 1469-72 church accounts suggesting a jaunt with the word
'jantacle' rather than a mere procession and Carew's account of a mock
court affording a glimpse of sports at Halgavor. Secondly, as the word
'run' is deleted in favour of the word 'ride' in connection with the
silver shoes in the notes, we know beyond all doubt that there was
horse racing for prizes during the Riding. This, coupled with the
mayoral entertainment of the gentry in 1691 and 1707, was probably

the origin of the Bodmin Races which developed into a separate
county event later in the 18th century. It could also link the Riding
with pagan games of the 6th century for, in one of the earliest and
most authentic biographies of Welsh missionaries honoured in Cornwall
and Brittany, the "Life of St. Samson", it is recorded that horse
racing was part of *"the magical rites of their ancestors"*. St. Samson
came upon the games during the first half of the 6th century while
passing through the district of Trigg, in which Bodmin lies, after
having visited St. Kew monastery and before leaving for Brittany from
Golant. If, as must be suspected, the Riding has early origins, the
transcript of Samson's biography in G.H. Doble's "Saints of Cornwall",
book 5, pages 80-103 cannot be other than of the utmost fascination.
Bodmin is midway between St. Kew and Golant and its acknowledged
founder, Petroc, was by tradition an associate of St. Samson. (See
final note under 1803-1816).

1720

THOMAS COX, 'Magna Britannia et Hibernia', six volumes, London 1720-1731 (Cornwall Library, Truro: Ashley Rowe Collection, separately bound Cornwall section being pages 306-364 of volume one, 1720) - page 315

> *"In this town yearly, in the middle of July, is a kind of carnival kept, thousands of people coming to see the sports and pastimes. King Charles II honoured it with his company in his journey to Scilly and became a brother of the society, which it seems derives its original from the times before the conquest."*

NOTES

*Thomas Cox was Vicar of Bromfield in Essex, his publication *'collected and composed by an impartial hand'* being an extension of Camden's 'Britannia'. He agrees with Lhuyd as to the season in which the Riding was held but does not colour our interpretation of it by introducing Becket's Feast although, as a clergyman, we might expect him to use ecclesiastical terms. His description of a great concourse of people is reminiscent of Lhuyd's; and there is no mention of church but the Riding by now comprises a carnival and sports.

*Like Lhuyd, Cox mentions several Bodmin inhabitants as being over the age of ninety; it is therefore assumed that there were people alive when his publication appeared who could confirm or refute its contents. As far as may be ascertained, they were not in doubt until 1814 when the Lysonses published their 'Cornwall'.

*Charles II's *'journey to Scilly'* refers to his gradual movement westward for safety, while still Prince Charles during the Civil War, which culminated in his escape at 10 p.m. on March 2nd, 1646, aboard the 'Phoenix' from Land's End. As he is recorded as having been in Cornwall from July of 1645. there seems little reason to doubt that he attended the Riding then as described above. Hone's Year Book for 1821 recorded another tradition regarding the future King Charles II and Bodmin; passing through the town, he is reputed to have remarked that it was the politest place he had ever seen as one half of the houses appeared to be bowing and the other half uncovered - doubtless a wry observation on the devastation suffered as the result of Bodmin's having been his Cornish Royalists' centre for the four years up to 1646!

*Cox's account - written at least twenty years after the Riding is known to have lost its church connection - is obviously of the festival

as it was in his time, with the emphasis clearly on the sports. The
event, some 75 years before his writing, would probably have included
church attendance prior to its being banned during the Commonwealth .
However, this recollection of the auspicious occasion when the heir
apparent graced the Riding - and one which would obviously be more
noteworthy, than the usual church detail. to his informant - is of
importance. His use of the words *'brother'* and *'society'* lends this
reminiscence a semblance of truth for we know beyond doubt that
the Riding was originally organised by a society of brothers or guild.
*It may be noted that we have accepted Cox's account as being ob-
viously one of the Riding although he does not, in fact, name it such.
Our acceptance stems from the fact that his account is a natural
progression from Lhuyd's; but, had we never read the latter, we would
probably never have suspected that Cox's *'carnival in July'* could even
be related to, let alone a development of, the 15th century jaunt which
raised money and donated some to building funds, the 16th century
enforced church attendance of shoemakers, or the 17th century mayoral entertainment of the gentry. In fact, the only previous record, to
which we might have related Cox's account, is probably Carew's description of sports at Halgavor!
*Cox's comment, that the *'society'* organising the *'carnival'* apparently
originated in pre-Norman times, might well have prompted Iago's
deduction in 1903.

1750

ROBERT HEATH, 'A Natural & Historical Account of The Islands of Scilly & A Description of Cornwall', London 1750 (Cornwall Library, Truro: Local History Collection) page 445 -

> *"And a carnival is kept every year, about the middle of July, on Halgavor Moor near Bodmin, resorted to by thousands of people; the sports and pastimes of which were so well liked by King Charles II, when he touched there in his way to Scilly, that he became a brother of the jovial society. The custom of keeping up this carnival is said to be as old as the Saxons."*

NOTES

*Heath is described in the book as *"an officer of H.M. Forces sometime stationed in Scilly."*

*Dr. Couch, in his 1864 R.I.C. journal article, complained that *'Heath (and almost all our guide-books follow him) makes the Bodmin Riding identical with the Halgavor Sports; but with insufficient reason'* and *'says, without giving any authority,'* that the carnival was considered to be as old as the Saxons. Heath's authority was obviously Cox for, apart from his addition of Halgavor as the location, his account is practically identical to the latter's. We may only imagine that Cox obtained his record of Prince Charles' enjoyment of the sports from people alive when he wrote in 1720 who could recollect it; and that Heath observed, while serving in Cornwall, that the custom still continued and was held at Halgavor - hence their reference to no other authorities. It should be pointed out, however, that Heath does **not** make the Riding identical with Halgavor Sports for he does not mention the former; but Dr. Couch does, although he maintains that the two are separate, for by accepting that Heath's account of sports at Halgavor is also one of the Riding **he** equates the two!

*The word *'carnival'*, as used by both Cox and Heath, originally denoted a festivity held during Shrovetide before the fasting of Lent.

1812

A LETTER FROM WALTER RALEIGH GILBERT OF BODMIN PRIORY TO THE REVEREND DANIEL LYSONS, JULY 11th, 1812 (British Library Department of Manuscripts, London: Add. Ms. 9417, folio 186 recto and verso) -

"Sir - In answer to your enquiries I beg to inform you that a ceremony (now vulgarly called Bodmin Riding) has been observed with great notoriety, till within 20 or 30 years, since which it has dwindled into mere revelry and the original meaning forgotten. It was always regulated by the nearest Sunday to Thomas a Becket's martyrdom, on which day they appeared at church with ribbons etc. to denote the approaching fete. On Monday, a grand procession of the principal inhabitants, formed into classes with the emblems of their trades and professions, took place, preceded by music, drums etc., and two men, one with a garland, the other a pole ornamented with flowers, ribbons, etc. etc. which they had previously deposited at the Priory and from whence they received it from the hands of the Master of the House as representing the Prior. They then proceeded to celebrate their sports and games. Mrs. Gilbert has conversed with some of her ancestors who remembered when the gentlemen of the neighbourhood sent presents to them and attended the ceremony; and I myself have presented the garlands and subscribed to their sports since I have been in possession of these premises."

NOTES

*W.R. Gilbert, the fourth son of Captain Pomeroy Gilbert of Compton Castle in Devon, was 60 years of age when he replied to Daniel Lysons's enquiries regarding details for his forthcoming 'Cornwall'. And there may be some justification for Maclean's later complaint that that work was *"based too much upon local information contributed . . by some half a dozen Cornish gentlemen, hence relying rather upon tradition . . than original research"* for at least two points in the letter above could mislead. The first would be that Gilbert implied that the Riding had not always been known by that name whereas we know from earliest records that it had; and the second that he stated *'it was **always** regulated by the nearest **Sunday** to*

Becket's **martyrdom'** whereas his mention of that day is the first with which we have met and the apparent season of the Riding coincided with Becket's **translation** rather than his martyrdom in December.

*Deputy Lieutenant of Cornwall in 1782, Gilbert became a Gentleman of the Bedchamber to George III in 1820 and Colonel Commandant of the Cornwall Hussars Yeomanry Cavalry six years later. He was the second husband of the former Miss Nancy Hosken, the daughter of a Vicar of Bodmin who married into the local bellfounding Pennington family; and it was through Mrs. Gilbert's inheritance of the Priory estate from her uncle, William Pennington, that he came into possession of the property. The Pennington family had been in Bodmin since at least the 16th century, several members serving as mayor, and W.R. Gilbert continued that tradition by holding the office three times.

*As stated above, Gilbert described the Riding as it was in the 1780s and/or 1790s; and his impression that it had *'dwindled'* by the early 19th century coincided with accounts of others of that period while he agreed with Polwhele that its meaning had been forgotten.

*Gilbert's details of the church attendance, procession and sports are reminiscent of Lhuyd's a century earlier; but there are some differences and certain clarifications. The church association had obviously been restored some time during the 18th century; but, as all other writers mention Monday as being the commencement day of the Riding with the exception of Dr. Couch who appears to follow Gilbert's probably erroneous assertion that *'it was always regulated by the . . Sunday'*, we may imagine that, as Sunday had become 'church day' by that period, the revived Riding service was naturally held on that day rather than the Monday of Lhuyd's record. Even so, Gilbert's comments implied that people went to church gaily attired in readiness for the approaching festival, rather than to a special Riding service, in the 18th century.

*Apart from the Sunday, there are other details which seem new to us in Gilbert's account: drum music, a Priory visit, and a garland as well as a decorated pole. As far as the music is concerned, Dr. Couch in 1864 had it analysed and it was suspected to have derived from the French revolutionary air; should such a suspicion be confirmed, it is likely that the music was introduced into the Riding proceedings by French officers paroled in Bodmin during the 1780s and 1790s. The Priory visit also was probably a late addition to the festival possibly in the 17th, but more likely in the 18th, century after the church attendance had been discontinued by Lhuyd's time; William Pennington had rebuilt the Priory House from about 1765 and, as an influential local gentleman and member of the corporation, it is possible that he encouraged and patronised the Riding in the manner described at the end of the letter above and that Gilbert continued the tradition, the Riding visiting the House - and also other residences according to C.S. Gilbert - rather as Padstow's 'Obby 'Oss pays a courtesy call upon Prideaux Place today. It would also seem that, after flowers and greenery had been collected from the countryside, as described by Polwhele, they were deposited at the Priory to be made up into the ceremonial garland and decorated pole for presentation during the visit. It must be remembered, however, that Lhuyd clearly stated that **one** garlanded **pole** was originally carried to church en route to the sports and one wonders if this would have once been the rod erected when the borough or guild court was in session as was the custom, this would explain the carrying of the timber and also connect with the Halgavor mock court tradition. The 'riding' of effigies on poles (6th paragraph, Appendix 4) might also be considered in this respect however.

*The mention, in the letter above, of neighbouring gentry sending presents and subscribing to the sports is reminiscent of what happened at the Bodmin Races described under the dates 1823, 1824, 1825 - the latter probably continuing the custom after the Riding had lost the support of the 'principal inhabitants'. The passage also sheds some light on Mayor May's entertaining the gentry with wine in 1691 and Mr. Robartes's gift of venison in 1707.

*Gilbert's description, of the Priory House master 'representing the Prior', is the first; and it is difficult to decide between its being a genuine tradition or an assumption similar to Couch's regarding the Riding stewards and church - ale wardens.

1803-1816

**RICHARD POLWHELE, 'The History of Cornwall',
seven volumes from 1803; volume one, revised 1816,
pages 46 & 47 -**

> *"There is a festival still celebrated in Bodmin which is
> called the Bodmin-riding; deducible, perhaps, from
> the pagan worship of the goddess of flowers, though
> now retaining a stronger tincture of saintly super-
> stition. It is held in the month of July, on the Monday
> after St. Becket's day; when the common people
> ride out into the country; and returning, proceed
> to the Priory with garlands of flowers; which they
> there present, according to immemorial usage.
> Why they make this procession to the Priory and
> present their flowers, few of them know: they
> only know that their forefathers had done the same.
> But there is little doubt that the offering of flowers
> was at the shrine of Thomas a Becket; and that
> the saint had the honour of superseding some
> pagan deity."*

NOTES

*Vicar of Manaccan in later years, Polwhele was born in the Truro
area in 1760.

*His seven-volume work appeared in the period 1803-1808; and in
1816 a corrected and enlarged edition was published. The passage
above occurs in his review of folklore and customs; and, in a footnote
on page 54 of volume 3, he dealt again with Bodmin traditions
quoting Carew's and Heath's descriptions of Halgavor Sports.

*From the passage above it may be seen that Polwhele followed Lhuyd
and Gilbert in mentioning the proximity of Becket's Day to the Riding's season, although, as we have noticed, the other clergyman, Cox,
did not. But he corroborated Lhuyd's Monday as the day of commencement rather than Gilbert's Sunday; and described participants as
"the common people" rather than *"principal inhabitants"* as mentioned by the latter reporter.

*Evidently the Riding continued into the 19th century; and the
Priory visit seems to have been so strongly established by the time
Polwhele wrote that he understood it to be *"according to immemorial
usage".* As this appears to make little sense when our first recorded
mention of that part of the procedure is Gilbert's, it is probably an
example of the way in which the "Riding saga" developed as one

antiquary copied another (see 4th note under 1939).

*From Polwhele we learn that the Riding flowers were collected by riding into the countryside; and it seems that the church attendance had once again been discontinued. But whether or not music and sports were still parts of the procedure, we are not told.

*Polwhele it was who introduced the idea that the Riding might have derived from a pagan flower rite which was transformed into a veneration of St. Thomas Becket. This was picked up by subsequent antiquaries such as C.S. Gilbert and Drew so that the Roman Floralia was seriously considered as an origin by the time Dr. Couch wrote in 1864. Bodmin has, of course, Roman connections by virtue of the imperial garrison of the first century at Nanstallon; but, as Dr. Couch noted, if the Riding was a Midsummer festival it is more likely to have stemmed from a native rather than a Roman ceremony. It seems more probable that the races of the Riding sports, as noticed under the date 1700, are the direct link with the pagan past. Nevertheless, our festival assumed some kind of religious significance for, although there is little hint of a saint's feast in the earliest remaining records, Lhuyd termed it a *"feast"* in 1700. Polwhele's assumption that the Riding is an instance of a pagan rite being adopted by Christianity is probably fair enough; but why Becket should supersede *"some pagan deity"* in a town so devoted to Petroc - patron of the Priory - remains a mystery and there seems no reason to believe that he did.

1814

DANIEL & SAMUEL LYSONS, 'Cornwall', published by Cadell c.1814; page 38 -

"Not far from Bodmin is a moor called Halgavor, where a kind of low festival called Bodmin Riding was formerly held annually in the month of July and attended by a great concourse of people: on this occasion there was elected a mock mayor . . . (Carew's description is quoted) *. . . It is probable that this custom was very ancient, and it is not unlikely that the Riding Guild before mentioned* (in connection with the rebuilding of the parish church) *had some connection with it.*
FOOTNOTE - Some remains of this custom still exist among the lower orders of people who make a procession on horseback carrying garlands . . . (W.R. Gilbert's letter to the Reverend Daniel Lysons, now Add. Ms. 9417, folios 186-188 in the British Library, is quoted; as is also Thomas Cox's account in 'Magna Britannia', 1720, to which the Lysonses add the comment:) *It may be observed that the season of the year in which Prince Charles journeyed towards the Scilly Isles does not accord with this tradition."*

NOTES

*Educated in Bath and sons of a Gloucestershire clergyman, the brothers Lysons compiled a "Magna Britannia" of which their 'Cornwall' was part; the first volume appeared in 1806 and the last in 1822. Samuel Lysons was a lawyer before becoming keeper of the Tower of London records in 1803; and his elder brother, Daniel, was a clergyman; he died in 1834, having survived Samuel by fifteen years.

*The Lysonses quoted Cox; but, as they also located the custom at Halgavor, either they were acquainted with Heath's account (or perhaps Polwhele's) or they gained information of that site for themselves. The latter is more likely as Maclean, in his preface, wrote *"Lysons's correspondence shows that he made much laborious enquiry";* and we have already reviewed W.R. Gilbert's letter to Daniel Lysons.

*The above account seems the first to draw attention to the Riding Guild of the parish church accounts and to connect it with the festival. The manuscript had apparently been discovered in a room above the south porch of the church in about 1750 but it was not until about 1807 that it was removed to the guildhall for examination.

*It will be noticed that the Lysonses stated that the Halgavor part of the proceedings was *"formerly"* held; but that only a mounted procession with garlands enjoyed by the *"lower orders"* existed by the time they wrote. This seems to agree with Polwhele's account slightly earlier, although not completely - regarding the Halgavor aspect - with C.S. Gilbert's record slightly later. But, from all three, it may be gathered that the Riding was dying as a town event during the first quarter of the 19th century.

*The brothers' comment, that *"the season of the year in which . . Charles journeyed towards the Scilly Isles does not accord"* with the tradition that he attended the Riding, is valid if the actual voyage in March is meant, whereas the Riding took place in July. We have shown however, under the date 1720 that the Prince's journeying *'towards'* the Isles brought him into Cornwall during July of 1645.

*The Lysonses were probably (inadvertently) responsible for the Riding's being made *'identical with Halgavor sports'* about which Dr. Couch complained and for which he blamed Heath. As we have noticed, it was Polwhele who linked the accounts of Carew and Heath in his third volume; and the Lysonses seem to have developed that idea in the passage above.

1820

CHARLES SANDOE GILBERT, 'An Historical Survey of Cornwall', published by Longman 1820; volume two, page 634 -

*"On a moor called Halgavor, a little to the west of the
town, is held a kind of annual festival called Bodmin
Riding; and although the rough original amusements
of the day are much reduced, they are not wholly extinct.
We are informed by Carew that, on this occasion it was
customary for the inhabitants to form on the moor a
mock court . . .* (Carew's description is quoted; as is
also W.R. Gilbert's letter to Daniel Lysons, 1812) . . .
*at present the lower classes of inhabitants form a kind
of procession on horseback carrying garlands, etc., and
after having paid respects to the monastery of St. Benets
and other neighbouring places, return again to the town
to conclude the festivity of the day. The origin of these
customs is said to have arisen from a devotedness to the
shrine of Thomas a Becket."*

NOTES

*Born at Kenwyn near Truro in 1760, C.S. Gilbert eventually became
a pharmacist. His 'Survey', the first volume of which appeared in
1817, was the result of a study of history in order to discover whether
or not he was connected with the Gilbert family of Compton Castle
in Devonshire.

*By the time of his writing, the 19th century version of the Riding
had been established sufficiently for him almost dutifully to reproduce
Carew's description and W.R. Gilbert's letter to Daniel Lysons and to
mention Polwhele's Becket theory. His account raises three important
points, however.

*The first is that he mentioned Halgavor as being to the *'west of the
town'*, whereas the Moor is now to the south-east of Bodmin. He
could just have written 'west' in error for 'east' or mistaken the West
Heath for Halgavor Moor; but, in any case, the apparent confusion as
to the location of the Riding sports is worthy of review.

Lhuyd in 1700 described them as being held on *'Bodmin downs'* which,
by the time of Maclean's writing in the 1870s, would have been understood as the Racecourse. However, as the West Heath proper is the
area now occupied by St. Lawrence's Hospital and the 1837 Boundaries Commission Report map designated the Beacon and lands to
its west and south 'Bodmin Downs', it would seem that Halgavor

Moor embraced a much larger area than it does today and part of it - which might be described as being *'a little to the west of the town'* - was known as Bodmin Downs. This would explain why Carew's Halgavor Sports were incorporated in Riding descriptions by writers for, to them, events taking place at the same time and venue as the Riding would obviously have been part of it. We therefore have the possibility of a site being recorded in 1602 by Carew, in the 18th century by Cox and Heath, seemingly by Gilbert in 1820 and by John Burton in 1905 as a perpetual and traditional venue of the Riding sports - the Beacon. Presumably, when the Races - as we suspect - broke away from the Riding sports, they were held at a different site, the Racecourse, which continued to be the location even when they rejoined the sports in the mid-19th century. All reports would now seem to agree, with the exception of Dr. Couch's which located the sports at Town End; but as, by this, he might have meant West Heath, there is every likelihood that the Bodmin Downs part of Halgavor Moor - all that is left of which is the Beacon - was one site referred to by different descriptions.

*The second point is that Gilbert mentioned that the *'Halgavor amusements'* were *'not wholly extinct'.* This would seem to conflict with the Lysonses' and Drew's accounts which inferred that Halgavor events had been discontinued during the first quarter of the 19th century. Whether or not Gilbert actually witnessed the Riding and sports personally - or they were revived at the time of his investigations - is unclear. Dr. Couch, writing some forty years after Gilbert, stated that *'no remembrance of Halgavor **Court** exists among people now resident in the area',* which might imply that other sports still took place.

*The third point concerns Gilbert's mention of the visit to *'the monastery of St. Benets and other neighbouring places'.* St. Benets at Lanivet was founded by parishioners in 1411 as a leper house, rather than a monastery, and the chapel, only the tower of which still exists, was added later in the 15th century; siezed by the Crown in 1545, the house subsequently became a private residence. There seems little reason to doubt that this visit was made during the ride into the countryside which is mentioned by other writers, although Gilbert implies that garlands were **taken** to rather than collected from there. In fact, such a visit would support the view that the Riding participants paid courtesy calls upon members of the gentry who sponsored and attended the festivities (see 5th note under 1812).

1824

'THE HISTORY OF CORNWALL' compiled by FORTESCUE HITCHINS and edited by SAMUEL DREW; volume one.

1) *page 720 -*
"A carnival which had been held for ages on Halgavor Moor near Bodmin, of which Carew gives the following account, is generally thought to have originated with the Saxons... (Carew's description is quoted) *... This carnival always took place in the middle of July; and, from the manner in which the process was conducted, it gave rise to a proverbial expression, applied to any person seen in dirty apparel - 'he deserves to be presented in Halgavor Court'."*

2) *page 722 -*
"At Bodmin there is still celebrated a festival which is called Bodmin Riding; which, from the manner of the procession, is probably deducible from the pagan worship of the goddess of flowers. But it has degenerated from the design of its primitive institution, being now strongly tinctured with papal superstition. It always takes place in July, on the Monday following the day of Thomas a Becket, in whose honour it seems to be ignorantly continued. The people, mounted on horses and asses, ride into the country; and, after collecting garlands of flowers, they return and proceed to the Priory where they present them according to ancient custom. There can be no doubt that this offering of flowers was at the shrine of Thomas a Becket, which saint has had the honour of superseding the pagan deity."

NOTES

*Samuel Drew was a self-taught metaphysician of the St. Austell area, where he was born in 1765. A shoemaker by trade and also a local preacher and avid reader of politics and philosophy, he took over 'The History of Cornwall' upon Hitchens's death; and, although described as its editor, most of the work is his.

*From the words *'Halgavor'* and *'Saxon'* in the first passage above, it is evident that his source was Heath; but, as he also quoted Carew, he was probably following Polwhele's footnote on page 54 of the third volume. Thus, instead of *'guide books'*, such as Drew's 'History' if it may be termed such, following Heath as Dr. Couch complained, it is

more likely that they followed Polwhele; this would explain why Drew dealt with the Riding and Halgavor Sports separately, despite Couch's assertion that only Carew made *"independent mention"* of the Sports.
*Our suspicion that Drew used Polwhele as a source is confirmed in the second passage above for it is, almost verbatim, the latter's description reproduced. The only differences appear to be that Drew clarified the mounts upon which the people rode; and that, whereas the Anglican clergyman, Polwhele, wrote that the Riding was *'tinctured with* **saintly** *superstition',* the local preacher, Drew, used the word *'papal'.*
*Drew agreed with the Lysonses by putting Halgavor Sports in the past tense - which seems to confirm our suggestion that C.S. Gilbert incorrectly assumed that *"they are not wholly extinct"* - and with all the writers of the early 19th century in describing the Riding as still existent, although in degenerate form. From all accounts it is apparent that the sporting side of the Riding had more or less died by this period; it therefore seems probable that Halgavor Sports, including the mock court, were originally part of the festivities and that the 'carnival' was the mounted procession thereto.
*It is noticeable that the Lysonses refutation in 1814 of Prince Charles's visit seems to have been accepted so that later writers made no mention of it until Dr. Couch wrote in 1864.

1823, 1824, 1825

CORNISH NEWSPAPER REPORTS (Royal Institution of Cornwall Museum, Truro)

WEST BRITON newspaper; Friday, July 2 1824 reports -

1) *"A correspondent requests us to state that a considerable sensation has been excited throughout the county by a report, we hope unfounded, that it is not intended to hold the usual races at Bodmin this year and that the posts have been removed from the course . . . we hope no private feelings will be allowed to interfere with an amusement which brings together . . . gentlemen from all parts of the county."*

2) *"We are informed that the celebration of the ancient festival of Bodmin Riding, which for some time past has been on the decline, will this year be revived with all the spirit of former days. The games, including wrestling, ringing, etc. will be on an unusually extensive scale; and wrestling, it is supposed, will afford the best sport which has been witnessed in this county for many years, there being ten sovereigns for the best man and five shillings for every standard, with other prizes in proportion. The Riding will be held on Monday, Tuesday and Wednesday, the 19th, 20th and 21st of July."*

ROYAL CORNWALL GAZETTE newspaper; Saturday, July 24 1824 reports -

3) *"BODMIN RIDING - the anticipations of the amateurs of athletic sports, relative to the revival of the ancient festivity of Bodmin Riding, have been fully realised. The value of the prizes and the spirit with which those who had the direction of the amusements exerted themselves, drew together a concourse of people greater than was remembered on any similar occasion. The sports commenced on Monday with wrestling: Henry Maberly of Cardinham bore off the 1st prize, a gold laced hat; the 2nd prize was gained by Thomas Sleeman of St. Tudy.*
The sports of the second day commenced with a trial of skill in ringing. The 1st prize, £6, was won by the ringers of Egloshayle; the 2nd prize, eight fine hats, by the ringers of St. Kew; the 3rd prize, a silver cup, by the

*ringers of St. Tudy; and the 4th prize, eight favours, by
the ringers of Blisland.
The 1st prize for wrestling this day, ten sovereigns, was won
by Jory of St. Kew; the 2nd prize, five sovs, and the 3rd
prize, two sovs, were divided between Lovering of St.
Columb and Broad of Simonward by a decision relative
to the rules of wrestling; the 4th prize, one sov, was
obtained by Kent of Gwennap. The standards made
were twenty-four and received five shillings each.''*

1825

WEST BRITON newspaper; Friday, July 29. 1825 reports -

*4) "We are sorry to find the Bodmin Races are likely to be
postponed for another year. In consequence of this
circumstance, some gentlemen in our neighbourhood
have subscribed for a silver cup to be run for near Truro.
We expect to be able to give arrangements for the intended
race in our next publication."*

WEST BRITON; Friday, August 5. 1825 advertisement -

*5) "TRURO RACES, 1825" - proposed to commence with
wrestling on Monday, August 29th; the racing to take
place on Tuesday, August 30th to be followed by a ball
in the Assembly Rooms.*

NOTES

*Report 1 above concerns the Bodmin Horse Races which were held
annually on Cardinham and Bodmin Downs, the winning post and
principal stand being near Council Barrow on the latter, until discontinued in 1790 as the result of an election quarrel between county
families. Resumed in 1806 through the influence of Bodmin's patron,
Lord (Francis Basset) de Dunstanville, the course was then wholly on
Bodmin Downs with the stand and winning post near Holton Gate.
Tavern facilities were available, probably at the present Racecourse
or Six Chimneys Farmhouse, and there were evening balls, presumably
in the hall of the old friary church then on Mount Folly. Apparently,
when the gentry were able to travel abroad again after the French
Wars, interest in these county races gradually waned. An advertisement appeared on the front page of the West Briton for July 4
1823 outlining forthcoming events - "First Day: the best of 3 two-mile

heats, all ages, for a plate of £50 presented by the county M.P.s; ditto, non-thorough-breads, for a sweepstake of 5 guineas each; ditto for the Ladies' Plate of £50, winner for sale if claimed within 15 minutes of the race: runner-up's owner to have first refusal, price 200 guineas. Second Day: 4 miles for a gold cup valued at 100 guineas; Handicap Plate of £50 presented by de Dunstanville for undistanced beaten horses. Entries at the Racecourse Inn before 6 p.m. the day prior to commencement; riders and colours to be named; booths and smiths only by leave of the clerk; all dogs on the course to be destroyed; Races commence at 11 a.m. with half-an-hour between heats." (Paraphrased & abridged). From report 1 above, however, it seems that *private feelings* once again stopped the races from being held in 1824.

*The date of the Races varied from August 22nd and 23rd in 1809 according to the Taunton Courier, to September 1st and 2nd by 1819 when they were altered to September 7th and 8th so as not to clash with shooting, according to the West Briton; and in 1823, according to the abovementioned advertisement in the latter newspaper, they took place on August 27th and 28th. When, in 1824, the Races were cancelled for some reason, the Riding was revived in *"the spirit of former days"* and held later in July than had been usual - on the 19th, 20th and 21st. It may be of interest to review the connection between the Riding and Races from the time of Lhuyd in 1700.

*In that period, the church service having been discontinued, the emphasis was on the sports which included *"riding for silver shoes on Bodmin Downs"* on the two Mondays after July 7th. This would extend the proceedings well into July, hence probably Cox's and Heath's timing events *"in the middle of July."* By 1790, when the Races were discontinued, the Riding church service had been revived; but by 1806, when the Races resumed, the Riding had declined and lost its church connection. With 1824 came another discontinuation of the Races but a revival of the Riding with a marked emphasis on the sports; moreover, as though continuing the Races' tradition, there was on *"the evening of the second day of the sports . . a grand ball for the servant girls and their followers, which was kept up until 8 or 9 o'clock the next morning"*, according to Mr. Hamilton Jenkin ('Cornwall & Its People', David & Charles, 1970).

*From report 3 above, it is evident that the Riding in 1824 was a county event like the discontinued Races, drawing a *"concourse of people"* from as far away as Gwennap despite there being no smooth roads nor railways at that time. *"Favours"*, mentioned in connection with the ringing, were the equivalent of our rosettes; prize money may be expressed in present-day terms as follows: *'sovereign'* = £1 gold coin; *'five shillings'* (5/-d) = 25p. *'Simonward'*, from whence came a winning wrestler, was St. Breward; and a *'standard'*, in wrestling, entailed the throwing of two men during a contest or the throwing of one and standing for a specified time with another.

*Reports 4 and 5 above indicate that, when Bodmin Races were cancelled for a second year running, Truro filled the gap in the 1825 Cornish calendar; and it is noticeable that, although not as rich an occasion as Bodmin's with its gold cup and handsome prizes, Truro Races as advertised included the wrestling, riding and ball traditional to the former county event and Riding at Bodmin. Races at the latter town resumed in 1833 and (Lt.-Gen.Sir) Walter Raleigh Gilbert ensured their continuance until he left for India about 1840; but, even after that year, they were occasionally held during the Riding when he was home on leave, according to John Burton's 1905 recollections. With Gilbert's death in 1853, however, they ceased.

*Dr. Couch, in his 1864 R.I.C. journal article, mentioned having in his possession *"a deprecatory pamphlet dated 1825 entitled 'A Letter To A Friend, relative to the approaching games commonly called Bodmin Riding'."* By this year, it is evident that the festival was thought of as 'games' and not particularly favourably by at least one person! This poses the question, however, as to whether or not the revived Riding in 1824 included the mounted procession and anything other than sports. The press reports stated that the Riding was to be held on three days yet recorded the events of the first two only so that the Wednesday could have been the day of the Riding proper; and also we have the account of Drew. The latter however, although published in 1824, was obviously written prior to that year; and, in any case, it was so close to Polwhele's as to appear suspiciously like a copy of it rather than the result of personal research or observation. Nevertheless, as we noticed under Carew's passage and under the dates 1691 and 1700, the Riding comprised several elements, only one or two of which appealed to particular reporters upon whom we rely for details. We may, therefore, only guess if or when some parts were added to or left out of the whole procedure. The apparent change of date in 1824 **is**, however, of interest for, had Lhuyd not mentioned (probably incidentally) the proximity of Becket's Day to the Riding's commencement, we may have been content to accept as the correct timing 'the middle of July' as stated by Cox and Heath. This could well tally with the 1691 mayoral account entry and with Lhuyd's 'second Monday after July 7th'; we would then consider later accounts centred around Becket as being those of 19th century 'purists' intent upon fitting the Riding tidily into the patronal feast category.

*It might be marked that the Bodmin Downs, mentioned in the first note of this section, refers to the Racecourse area. (For Bodmin Downs, of the Halgavor area, please see pages 33-34).

1864

THOMAS QUILLER COUCH, 'Popular Antiquities - Bodmin Riding & Halgavor Sports', Royal Institution of Cornwall journal, volume one, number two, October 1864, pages 56-60 –

"I shall begin with a festival of which remembrance lingers only among people past middle-age, and which is never likely to be revived. It was kept at Bodmin on the Sunday and Monday after St. Thomas a Becket's day, July 7th. A puncheon of beer having been brewed in the previous October, and duly bottled in anticipation of the time, two or more young men who were entrusted with the chief management of the affair; and who represented 'the wardens' of Carew's church-ales, went round the town attended by a band of drums and fifes or other instruments. The crier saluted each house with: 'To the people of this house, a prosperous morning, long life, health, and a merry riding!' The musicians then struck up the Riding Tune, a quick and inspiriting measure, said by some to be as old as the feast itself. The householder was solicited to taste the Riding ale, which was carried round in baskets. A bottle was usually taken in, and it was acknowledged by such a sum as the means or humour of the townsman permitted, to be spent on the public festivities of the season. Next morning, a procession was formed, all who could afford to ride mounted on horse or ass, first to the Priory, to receive two large garlands of flowers fixed in staves, and then in due order through the principal streets to the Town-end, where the games were formally opened. The sports, which lasted two days, were of the ordinary sort: wrestling, foot-racing, jumping in sacks, etc. It is worthy of remark that a second or inferior brewing, from the same wort, was drunk at a minor merry-making at Whitsuntide. This description of the ceremony has been obtained from those who took part in its latest celebration.
No one who compares this account of the Riding with Carew's description of church-ales, can doubt that the two were originally identical in their meaning . . . .
(the parish church rebuilding accounts, shoemakers' order, and Polwhele are quoted).
I have heard an opinion that the feast was in celebration of the restitution of St. Petroc's bones . . . . (Heath and the

1825 deprecatory pamphlet are quoted).
I have heard some doubts expressed as to the antiquity of the Riding Tune . . . " (Dr. Couch proceeded to record William Sandys' opinion that it resembled tunes of the late 17th or 18th centuries; and Chappel's that it was founded on the 'Fall Of Paris' which, according to Sandys, derived from the French revolutionary air 'Ca ira'. He then mentioned Heath's account of Charles II's alleged participation in the Riding at Halgavor, and the Lysonses' doubting its authenticity; and finally discussed Carew's description of the Halgavor Sports). *Several attempts have been made to resuscitate this festival* (Bodmin Riding); *but it is now hopelessly dead."*

NOTES

*Dr. Thomas Quiller Couch was the son of the former Miss Jane Quiller and Dr. Jonathan Couch of Polperro. He married Mary Ford of the Newton Abbot area; and settled in Bodmin as a medical practitioner. Sir Arthur Thomas Quiller-Couch, the famous Man of Letters, was born to them in the town a year before the above appeared in print.

*Reference to other parts of the article may be found under the dates 1602, 1750, 1812, 1803/16, 1820, 1824, 1823/5, 1903, 1905, 1928 and 1939 in this book. The journal in which the paper appeared may be consulted at the Cornwall Museum, Truro.

*It would seem, from the above, that Dr. Couch obtained his details from those *'past middle-age'* in 1864 as they were, according to him, the only people who could remember the festival which was *'never likely to be revived'*. How then, it might be asked, could John Burton recollect in 1905 the Riding in the 1840s and 1850s, W.J.P. Burton in 1928 remember events of the 1860s and Dr. Couch's own son in 1939 reminisce about the festival as it was in the 1870s? One may only assume that the rather boisterous procession which annually passed Couch's house - in Pool Street when he wrote and later in Fore Street - was not considered by him to be remotely connected with the sedate and orderly Riding he described as an academic!

*The *"Sunday and Monday after St. Thomas a Becket's Day"* affords the clue to one of Couch's, albeit unacknowledged, sources of information for the only writer we have discovered as mentioning the Sunday is W.R. Gilbert in 1812. From our reading of the above, it would appear that the ale ceremony took place on the Sunday; and that Couch's 'past middle-aged' informant in 1864 could not remember attendance at church during the Riding. This seems strange in view of John Burton's statement in 1905 that the corporation proceeded to church in his youth, the period immediately prior to Couch's writing the article; but, as Burton referred to a Monday, it was presumably

discounted by Couch.
*The account of the ale ceremony seems to be the first and, although
it is coloured by Couch's allusions to Carew's church-ales in the hope
that we shall agree that they and the Riding were identical, it is of
interest. The only previous mention of alcohol connected with the
Riding was in the 1691 mayoral accounts concerning wine for the
gentry; as, however, John Burton stated that *'inhabitants had the
privilege of brewing beer for this annual occasion'*, we may take it
either that the custom developed when the 'lower orders' were left
to their own devices by the end of the 18th century, in emulation of
the wine-swilling of their 'betters' in former times, **or** that a genuine
ale custom had passed through the ages with the Riding unrecorded.
In any event, it had apparently become the method of fund-raising
for the event by the 19th century.
*The *"drum and fife band"* details, together with the music which
followed Couch's article and is also printed in the centre pages of this
book, clarified the brief mention in W.R. Gilbert's account and
showed how and when accompaniment was used during the Riding.
*Having stated that the Riding took two days, the Sunday and Monday,
Couch proceeded to describe three days' events: the Sunday ale
ceremony, the Monday procession and two-day sports. It may also be
noticed that, whereas Lhuyd described one garlanded pole and W.R.
Gilbert mentioned a garland besides, Couch stated that two garlanded
staves were received from the Priory. As for the seeming disagreement
regarding the venue of the sports, please see under the date 1820.
*The *'second or inferior brewing . . drunk at a minor merry-making at
Whitsuntide'* is, as Couch suggested, *'worthy of remark'*. Whit and
Rogation Sundays are but a fortnight apart, the former being the
seventh Sunday after Easter and the latter the fifth. Rogation week
was the traditional bounds' beating time, and, in view of the comments
of W.J.P. Burton and John Stephens in the 1928 Guardian, it would
seem that there was some link between that event and the Riding.
In the appendices, it may be seen that Bath's mock king ceremony in
honour of Edgar took place at Whitsuntide as also did the Liskeard
Riding; details of the latter are particularly relevant in connection
with Bodmin's *'minor merrymaking'* as, at Liskeard, similar events
took place *'on several market days and the fair day before the games'*.
*Couch quoted the Shoemakers' Order of 1583 which, by the time of
his writing, had been published in Wallis's 'Bodmin Register'; and
mentioned that the Riding had been considered as a celebration of
the return of Petroc's relics to Bodmin from Brittany, whither they
had been taken by a thief, in 1176/7. This seems to have been siezed
upon by subsequent antiquaries and often repeated so that it, along
with so much else, became part of the Riding saga! It has now been
established, however, that Petroc's bones were restored to Bodmin on

the Feast of the Holy Cross, September 14;and, as neither that date
nor the dates of the Saint's death, June 4th, and of his translation,
October 1, have ever as far as is known coincided with the Riding, it
is unlikely that the festival had any connection with Bodmin's early
missionary. (But see Appendix 8).

*It is difficult to determine the period of the Riding Couch purported
to have described in 1864. Were it a procedure followed in the youth
of those *'past middle-age'* in that year, it might have been the revival
of 1824 for those who could recollect that in 1864 would have been
50 years of age or more; yet, apart from the wrestling, which would
have taken place in the Beacon pit mentioned by John Burton in
1905 rather than at Town End as mentioned by Couch surely, the
sports described in the article above do not correspond with those
mentioned by the 1824 press. Also, the dates of the 1824 revival,
Monday, Tuesday and Wednesday: July 19, 20 and 21, are different
from Couch's *'Sunday and Monday after'* Becket's Day. And further-
more, from all other early 19th century accounts, we gather that the
Sunday church connection had disappeared by that period yet Couch
was so preoccupied with proving that the Riding and church-ales were
identical that he actually used the Sunday connection to prove his
point, quoting a 1570 sermon to support his contention that, as
church-ales took place on Sundays (unmentioned by Carew, Appendix
6) and so did the Riding, they were one and the same. In all, it seems
suspiciously as though Couch chose to ignore the Riding, albeit in
degenerate form, passing his door every year and to describe a festival
in 'pure' form - details of which were gleaned from recollection and
records - which had never really existed in such straight and interpret-
able detail at all.

*We are, therefore, forced to conclude that Couch's article is useful in
as far as it provides hitherto unrecorded detail of the ale ceremony, the
crier's salutation, the Whitsuntide merrymaking and sports venue and
an analysis of the Riding tune; but suspect regarding a firm date and
length of the festival, interpretations of its meaning, and in purporting
to be a *'description of the ceremony .. obtained from those who took
part in its latest celebration .. remembrance of which lingers only
among people past middle-age'.* Such a conclusion is important in that
Couch was widely quoted, either verbatim with acknowledgment or by
inference without, by such as Polsue in Lake's 'Cornwall' 1867,
Maclean in his 'Trigg Minor' 1870s, Wilkinson in his transcript of the
parish church accounts 1874 (which, in turn, was used by 'Lanje' and
Ashley Rowe in Guardian articles of the 1930s), by M.A. Courtney
in 1886/7, Iago in 1903, the writer of 'Whispers & Echoes' in the
Guardian for January 1930, by Irene Northan in the Western Morning
News for June 1973; and, spare her blushes, by the present writer as
reported in the Guardian for April 1967!

The Mayors present the Garlands to the Riding Stewards
(C.R. CLEMENS photo)

The Stewards of the Riding with the Garlands
(C.R. CLEMENS photo)

The Tasting of the Riding Ale Ceremonial
(C.R. CLEMENS photo)

*The Stewards of the Riding Ale with
Bombard & Blackjacks*
(C.R. CLEMENS photo)

School Dancers to the Riding Tune
(C.R. CLEMENS photo)

Junior Riding Entrants, Mount Folly
(C.R. CLEMENS photo)

Driving Entrant
(The Riding Cup Winner)

Senior Riding Entrants

The Mayoral Coach & Military Escort, Ring Road

The Band Plays the Riding Tune, Followed by Dancers

BODMIN RIDING

Above, is the Bodmin Riding tune which Dr. Couch had examined
by experts in 1864 and was thought to have derived from the French
Revolutionary air (see pages 41-44).

Described by Dr. Couch as a 'quick and inspiriting measure', the 3rd
line down is a repeat of the 8 bars in the top 2 lines.

BODMIN RIDING

Above, is the Bodmin Riding tune which was used at the 1974
revival. Several versions based upon this air exist, there being
slight variations in melody, key and tempo: hence its being
described as 'a stirring accompaniment for a march' by Iago and W.J.P.
Burton, while suggesting 'movements stately and dignified' to
Stephens (see page 56).

Walking Entrants, Dennison Road

Adult Riding Entrants

After the 'Barley Sheaf' Tasting & Before the 'Queens Head'!

Decorated Horse & Driving Entrants, Fore Street.

Rogationtide Riding, Bodmin Borough Bounds, 1923
Town Crier & Mayor, 1st & 3rd horseman respectively, on the right,
(by courtesy Mrs. E M Bound)

The Riding Wrestling Ring, Bodmin Beacon c. 1930
Immediately behind the ring is the 144ft. high Gilbert monument
(by courtesy: Mrs. M. Larsen)

1903

WILLIAM IAGO, 'Guide To Bodmin' published by Mate, unpaginated (Bodmin Reference Library; or Bodmin Museum: D.112) -

1) "Five of the Guilds - called in the (parish church re-building accounts) *manuscript 'the Ridyng Ildes' - kept up a festival on the Sunday and Monday nearest St. Thomas-a-Becket's day July 7. It is still called the Bodmin Riding. They performed their 'Janticle', processional jaunt, on horseback carrying emblems of their crafts and proceeded to the Priory where they received garlands on poles etc.; the masters, journeymen and apprentices were under the direction of a chosen steward. Other ceremonies and sports followed. It has been supposed by some that the festival may have been connected with the old Floralia, or else was a commemorative of the return of St. Petroc's relics, others consider that it had its origin in such proceedings as accompanied Church Ales in many places. A special air, called Bodmin Riding Tune, is well known in the town, and there is evidence of its having been in use during the last 140 years. It is a popular, stirring accompaniment for a march; its age and origin are unknown . . .*
In addition to Bodmin Riding, several other local observances prevailed. Halgavor Sports were also held in July. A mock mayor's court there and a Dragon Pit, a natural hollow on the moor, brought upon the unwary experiences that amused the onlookers. Viewing the Bounds was also carried out, at Rogationtide . . . "

2)" The suggestion that the figure (on the Bodmin borough seal) *represents King Edgar is supported by the fact that the festival called Bodmin Riding falls on King Edgar's Day, July 8, or as nearly as possible to it - the day after Thomas-a-Becket's translation - in the old English calendar. He was styled St. Edgar, King and Confessor, patron of monastic orders. "*

3)"(Referring to Bodmin's markets and fairs in existence in 1903:) *July 8, St. Edgar's Day, Anglo-Saxon King, Bodmin Riding, now scarcely observed. "*

NOTES

*Iago, who pronounced his surname 'eye-ay-go', was born in London in 1836 to Cornish parents; and, after graduating from Cambridge, served as chaplain to St. Lawrence's Hospital from 1862 until retiring in 1914, four years before his death. An archaeological gold medallist and sometime President of the Royal Institution of Cornwall, he was a widely quoted and prolific writer of articles on Cornish subjects, a much sought after illustrator of such works as Maclean's 'Trigg Minor', and in demand when something unusual was found or an ancient inscription needed deciphering.

*The three extracts above may be found in the text he contributed to Mate's guide whose pages are unfortunately not numbered although the entries above **are** numbered here for reference purposes in these notes.

*From extract 1 above, it will be seen that Iago was familiar with Couch's R.I.C. journal article in that he mentioned the Sunday and Monday nearest Becket's Day, the Floralia theory of Polwhele, the Petroc theory and Couch's church-ales idea but seemed to accept none of them. He appears, however, to have accepted that Couch had, as he claimed in the passage in his article dealing with the Riding tune, *'direct proof of its being in use at this festival for a century past'* for Iago's reference to evidence of the tune *'having been in use during the last 140 years'* would tally with Couch's assertion and extend the use of the tune back to the 1760s. As the first mention of music would seem to be W.R. Gilbert's and Couch's 'evidence' is not apparent, however, **our** earliest reference is to music in the 1780s or 1790s. There are several versions of the tune in various tempi so that opinions differ as to its form: Couch described it as *'a quick and inspiriting measure'*, Iago and W.J.P. Burton as *'a stirring accompaniment for a march'*, and Stephens thought it suggested *'movements stately and dignified, graceful and rythmic'* (see under the dates 1928 and 1930). From the final paragraph in the first extract above it may be gathered that Iago considered Halgavor Sports to be separate from the Riding although held in the same month.

*Extract 2 above is of immense interest to Bodmin historians for Iago seems to have been the first seriously to question the report of Leland in the 16th century that Bodmin regarded King Athelstan, 925-940, as its founder, benefactor and patron. As we note in Appendix 1 and under the date 1700, there is much to support a theory that the later Saxon king, Edgar, was or should have been celebrated by Bodmin. He was certainly a patron of Petroc's priory: he gilded the Saint's shrine in 963, he is the most mentioned monarch in the Bodmin Gospels which belonged to the monastery, and his emblem appears on

16th century Prior Vyvyan's mansion gateway and tomb. The prior
was overlord of Bodmin until the Reformation; and clerics, although
not permitted to be burgesses, could belong to guilds. Guildsmen
organised Bodmin Riding which took place *'right after St. Becket's
day'* July 7 - King Edgar's Day was July 8. The *'old English calendar'*,
to which Iago referred, was the Julian one dropped in 1752 in favour
of the Gregorian calendar. The Act establishing the latter, 24 Geo.
II c.23, provided that 1752 and ensuing years should begin on January
1 instead of March 25, that no year ending in OO should be a leap
year unless divisible by 400, and that September 2 of 1752 should be
followed by September 14 to effect the changeover. The resultant
'eleven lost days' altered the date of many a parish feast such as
Blisland's from September 11 to the 22. There is no evidence to
suggest that the Riding was similarly affected.

*Extract 3 above is yet another indication that Iago regarded Bodmin
Riding as King Edgar's Day, July 8; and what is also of interest is that,
even as late as in 1903, the festival appears to have been *'observed'*
however *'scarcely'*. Despite Iago's apparently considering the Riding
a separate event, one wonders if this surprisingly recent observance
had any connection with the custom *'observed in a degenerate form in
1904'* at Halgavor Moor as mentioned by Daniell in 1906.

1905

JOHN BURTON, 'Bygone Days In Bodmin'; The Guardian newspaper, March 24, page 4 (Bodmin Reference Library).

"Bodmin Riding took place on the second Monday in July. It was, no doubt, of pagan origin. I remember the Bodmin Teetotal Drum and Fife Band used to arouse us from our slumbers at 4 a.m. by promenading the streets until 8 o'clock playing the Bodmin Riding tune only, which still exists in Bodmin. At 10 o'clock the corporation and borough officials attended the parish church. In the afternoon sports, including wrestling, took place on the Beacon, where some of the best Cornish wrestlers took part (in the wrestling ring which still exists near the Gilbert column).

There was also a second day's wrestling. Booths and stalls were in abundance on the Beacon. When General Gilbert was home in Bodmin, horse racing used to take place on the racecourse. In the evening, the inhabitants, rich and poor, joined in the flora dance carrying garlands etc. through the streets accompanied by the band. 'Budley' Hicks generally led off the dance. The remainder of the week was kept up in jollification. The inhabitants had the privilege of brewing their own beer for this annual occasion without being interfered with in any way by the authorities, but this has long since been discontinued."

NOTES

*John Burton was one of several children of Joseph Burton who arrived in Cornwall from Stockport in 1830, set up a china and glass shop in Bodmin and married a Launceston girl, Miss Clemo. Fourteen years before his father's death in 1876, John Burton left the Bodmin home to hawk crockery around Falmouth; and, by 1865, he had opened what eventually became a famous curiosity shop at 27, Market Street in that town. He married, had eight children and, by his death in 1907, had become a very well known antiquarian and Cornish character.

*The passage above, contributed from Falmouth on March 3, 1905, described the Riding of Burton's youth in Bodmin prior to 1862. In fact, the horse racing *'when General Gilbert was home'* must have taken place before 1853 as the celebrated Lt. Gen. Sir Walter Raleigh Gilbert of the Sikh Wars died in that year.

*As far as Burton was concerned, the Riding began on *'the second*

Monday in July' and no other comment seemed necessary except to assume that it was *'of pagan origin';* his 'Monday' agrees with all other reporters with the exception of W.R. Gilbert, whose 'Sunday' might well have been correct for the revived church service at the end of the 18th century but was probably incorrect for the original and usual commencement day of the traditional feast.

*The *'Teetotal Drum and Fife Band'* is interesting in view of the beer comment but is reminiscent of the Roughtor Teetotal Revels when alcohol flowed in the 1840s (see my 'Bodmin Moor'); and we may be sure that Burton had his facts right as his father was a strict teetotaler. For the first time we learn how Bodmin was made aware of the arrival of Riding Day; and, with the exception of an actual 'riding', events of the first day would seem to have been traditional and even included church attendance at a civic service. When the latter was revived, after its lapse during the early 19th century, seems unknown but, whether by accident or design, it was placed on the Monday implied by Lhuyd as being customary prior to 1700.

*The Riding of Burton's youth would seem to have lasted for a *'week'* of *'jollification':* the first day being taken up with the early morning 'knocking up' and - according to W.J.P. Burton - tasting ceremonial, the 10 a.m. church service, the afternoon sports on the Beacon amid booths and stalls and occasional equestrian events on the Racecourse, and the evening flora dance; the second day with more wrestling; and the remainder of the week with general celebration. The *'Gilbert column'* mentioned as being on the Beacon would not have been there until 1856/7 when it was built to commemorate the General's achievements; the rare aerial photograph in this book shows its eventual position in relation to the *'wrestling ring'.* Burton's mention of horse racing during the Riding confirms the suspicions we have had that the Bodmin Races derived from the Riding sports, the *'booths and stalls'* being reminiscent of what we know about Racecourse events.

*Burton provided our first mention of the Beacon as being the site, already suspected by us, of the Riding sports; and also of the flora dance as being part of the festival, with participants *'carrying garlands'.* *" 'Budley' Hicks"* was born in Bodmin in 1808 and eventually ran his father's school until becoming governor of St. Lawrence's Hospital in 1848; during his mayoralty, 1865/6, he revived the beating of the bounds custom; and, apart from being renowned throughout the West Country as a wit and raconteur, he was obviously at the forefront of Bodmin's traditional events until his death in 1868. It is worth noticing that, in Burton's youth, the Riding seems to have been restored to its position as a town event patronised and enjoyed by the 'principal inhabitants', having suffered a decline and been continued only by the 'lower orders' between the 1790s and 1824 revival.

*The inhabitants' *"privilege of brewing their own beer . . without being* *interfered with"* is a thought-provoking comment in view of the fact that our only previous mentions of alcohol in connection with the Riding have been wine for the gentry in 1691 and Couch's ale ceremonial description in 1864. There seems every likelihood that the ale was introduced into the Riding fairly lately, perhaps during the 18th century.

*In the recollection of Burton above, we have a spontaneous description of a real folk festival which contrasts sharply with the academic pretensions of the early 19th century writers up to Couch. Had we little more than this glimpse of the festival as it was in the last century, we would still have the essentials with the exception of a mounted procession; in fact, we may have been far less confused about the details. But Burton's comparatively short article does pose questions in relation to Couch's account: why did the latter say that the Riding was *'now hopelessly dead'* in 1864 when the Burtons were enjoying an obviously very much alive event in that period; how could he state that it was *'kept on the Sunday and Monday'* when it began on the Monday and lasted a week; why were his informants *'past middle-age'* when he could watch the Riding from his windows in Pool Street and eventually in Fore Street; and so on? We may only conclude that the Ridings of the Burtons' young days were the *'several attempts made to resuscitate this festival'* mentioned by Couch and presumably considered by him to be pale imitations of various antiquaries' wishful thinking!

1906

J.J. DANIELL, 'A Compendium Of The History & Geography Of Cornwall', 4th issue edited by Thurstan C. Peter, 1906, page 323 -

" 'Take him before the mayor of Halgavor' is a Cornish proverb arising from an old custom of the people of Bodmin who used to assemble in confused multitudes on Halgavor Moor every year in July and elect a mayor of misrule and hold a mock trial for the punishment of petty offenders. The custom was observed in a degenerate form in 1904."

NOTES

*Daniell was master of Probus School and the first edition of his work appeared in 1854. It came to be known as "Collins's Cornwall" as the second and third issues were revised and rewritten by J.H. Collins by 1893.

*In the Guardian newspaper issue of September 8, 1911, page 3, a long and un-signed article entitled 'A Holiday Visit To Bodmin - History & Legend Revived' was carried. Included in it is a passage almost identical to that above with the exception that the words *'who were ducked in muddy water'* followed 'petty offenders'. If the custom was, in fact, observed as lately as in 1904, it had apparently changed very little in procedure since Carew's account was published in 1602.

1928

GUARDIAN NEWSPAPER ARTICLES. (Bodmin Reference Library)

1) FEBRUARY 2, page II: 'BODMIN 60 YEARS AGO - THEN & NOW - STRIKING CONTRASTS' BY COUNCILLOR W.J.P. BURTON -

"Every year on the Monday following St. Thomas' Day, July 7, the custom of observing some of the practices associated with Bodmin Riding was kept up. I should have regarded it as a neglect of duty if I did not make one of the crowd who assembled at the Turret Clock before it struck 4 on that particular morning; and often I acted as a diminutive member of the scratch band gathered together for the occasion. Precisely as the clock ceased striking the hour, the two preliminary beats of the big drum started the strains of the stirring old march known as Bodmin Riding, and, proceeding up Fore Street, the whole town was rudely awakened by the noise of a very mixed band and the noise of a vociferating crowd. Having disturbed the slumbers of Fore Street, Bore Street and Pool Street, the crowd dispersed for breakfast; but I fear that not all went to work. The band again turned out in the evening to lead the flora dance through the streets. A few well known characters usually danced in front of the band and caused great amusement by their antics."

2) APRIL 19, PAGE 13: 'BODMIN WHEN WE WERE BOYS & SOME TIME AFTER' BY W.J.P. BURTON AND JOHN STEPHENS.

"When we were boys, Rogationtide was regularly observed, not always by the beating of the borough bounds but, failing everything else, by the perambulations of the streets by a band in the early morning. The tune played, of course, was the Bodmin Riding with which everybody was familiar.

NOTES

*W.J.P. Burton was born in 1856 and, after spending his boyhood in Bodmin, was away from his home town for some 40 years until the 1920s. He then became a borough councillor; and addressed local organisations on former times, his lectures appearing as a booklet entitled 'History Of Bodmin' in 1925. In the autumn of 1928 he was elected mayor.

*His style is more formal than John Burton's; he was also influenced by past writers on the Riding as references to St. Thomas, above, and to Petroc's relics in other accounts suggest.

*The first passage above describes a Riding which took place at some time in the late 1860s: in fact, it seems to be a composite account of several such occasions. From his 'History' and from an article of his in the 'Old Cornwall' journal, volume VI, number 35, we learn that *"at this time the Sunday has already ceased to be an occasion, neither was there any proper organisation of the Monday's procession and sports . . . At 4 a.m. a rabble of boys and men . . marched up the main street halting at every public house . . where they were regaled with free drinks."* This gives an impression of Burton's being acquainted with Couch's article or W.R. Gilbert's letter in that he seems to think that the church service took place on a Sunday, whereas John Burton shows that it was part of the first day's, Monday's, proceedings. Nevertheless, we now know what Burton and the others of his 'rabble' were doing as they perambulated the town with the band - drinking!

*Writing to the Guardian issue, July 31, 1930, from the Isle of Wight, Burton named one of the characters who used to dance in front of the band at Rogationtide 'ridings.' In a subsequent issue, printed here under the date 1930, John Stephens described this local person, Eliza Tanner: she and the other *"well known characters"* who *"caused great amusement by their antics"* may be compared with the comic John and Joan of the Liskeard Riding.

*In the second passage above by Burton and his contemporary, Stephens, is the interesting recollection of a minor 'Riding' in place of the bounds' beating at Rogationtide, presumably during the 1860s or 1870s. This would probably be the *'minor merrymaking at Whitsuntide'* to which Dr. Couch referred in 1864. If we re-read accounts of Polwhele in 1803, the Lysonses in 1814, particularly of C.S. Gilbert in 1820, and of Drew in 1824, our suspicion that the Riding may have grown out of, or have been connected with, the ancient bounds' beating custom gains strength. Originally of religious as well as civic significance, the perambulation of the boundaries was observed on horseback and garlands as well as an effigy of a dragon were carried. The town crier or beadle announced "thus far extends the ancient borough of Bodmin" at certain landmarks and hurling played an important part in the proceedings. The mention of *"a ball of sylver"* in the Bodmin Parish and Borough Returns of 1552 (Maclean's "Trigg Minor", volume 3, page 420) is probably Cornwall's earliest record of the existence of a hurling ball. (See also Breton customs appendix).

*In Appendix 7, final note, we mention Burton's commenting that

Riding Day ended with a corporation dinner. This, referring to procedure in his youth during the 1860s, would seem to be a continuance of a custom implied by the 1691 mayoral accounts entry.

1930

GUARDIAN NEWSPAPER ARTICLES (Bodmin Reference Library)

1) January 16, Page 9: "Whispers & Echoes" -

"In connection with the Winter Festival of the Old Cornwall Societies it has been suggested, I see, that another attempt may be made to revive Bodmin Riding which Mr. T.Q. Couch 60 years ago wrote of as 'hopelessly dead'.
Bodmin Riding was held on the first Monday or Tuesday after July 7. Trades people of the town preceded by music and carrying emblems of their trades, walked in procession to the Priory. They were headed by two men, one with a garland and the other with a pole, which they presented and received back again from the master of the house as the then representative of the prior. The day before, two young men went around the town attended by a band of drummers and fifes . . . (Couch's account is followed).
Several attempts have been made to revive the Riding but they have all been unsuccessful."

2) August 7, Page 10: Letter from John Stephens, Eliot Lodge, Newquay -

"Mr. Burton mentioned Eliza Tanner who used to dance in front of the band on Rogation morning. Eliza was a well known character and for many years was recognised chief rag and bone gatherer in the town and district. True, she had a weakness for liquor but otherwise she was a hard working and industrious woman. She could often be seen returning from her rounds carrying a sack many men would hesitate to tackle.
A word in regard to the tune of Bodmin Riding. Unfortunately, this item is not included in Dr. Dunstan's Cornish music book recently published. Although Dr. Dunstan advertised extensively asking for local tunes , no-one sent him particulars of this one.
Apparently the tune was written for a processional dance which ought to be revived. Here is work for the Bodmin Old Cornwall Society during the ensuing winter. The music suggests movements stately and dignified, graceful and rythmic. The President of the Society, John Pethybridge, has I think the music in manuscript and the tune ought to be secured for posterity."

NOTES

*The title of the first passage above, 'Whispers & Echoes', was the name of the Guardian's editorial column at that time. It seems obvious that the writer was acquainted with W.R. Gilbert's 1812 recollection, as well as with Dr. Couch's 1864 article, for with the exception of his word *'walked'* the description above follows their accounts fairly closely. And even although he makes no mention of Sunday, which they would have as the Riding's first day, it is possibly implied in the writer's *'the day before (the first Monday or Tuesday after July 7)'*. One wonders if the *'several attempts . . to revive the Riding'*, mentioned by the columnist, were the events remembered by the Burtons but apparently discounted as true Ridings by Dr. Couch.

*Eliza Tanner, as described by Stephens in the second passage above, possibly explains Dr. Couch's and the first passage writer's apparent distaste for anything but a 'classic' Riding for she seems not to have been a member of 'town society'! Probably such as she came to the fore after the death in 1868 of Mayor Hicks who once led the evening flora dance.

*For other comments on the Riding Tune, please see under the date 1903.

1935

GUARDIAN NEWSPAPER EDITORIAL, 'Whispers & Echoes', May 2, page 9 -

"With the near approach of Silver Jubilee Day, towns and villages everywhere are putting the finishing touches to celebrations.

There was a proposal made at first that it might be possible to revive some of the old customs such, for instance, as the Bodmin Riding in the county town. In the end it was thought that this could hardly be revived successfully and that, in any case, it would not lend itself as was first thought to a successful broadcast over the air. I am afraid Bodmin Riding in olden days was very little other than a drunken spree. I never saw it myself but all that I have heard about it seems to suggest that opinion. It used to start in the small hours of the morning . . . (an account reminiscent of the Burtons' and others' is given) *. . . I have heard that on one occasion the drum was seen to be rolling away on its own down Chapel Lane.*

That sort of thing may have been possible 40 or 50 years ago but I don't think it could be successfully repeated today . . . . . . Beating the borough bounds, now, is another matter. That is an old custom which I think we must all be pleased is occasionally followed even in these more modern times."

NOTES

*It is evident from the passage above and from the first extract under the date 1930 that, whenever a special occasion had to be marked in Bodmin, the Riding was considered the most appropriate celebration. And, while attempts to revive the festival this century were apparently unsuccessful, the reason given for the 1935 failure is not without interest: *'it would not lend itself . . to a . . broadcast over the air'.* It may also be noticed that the editorial columnist mentioned events *'40 or 50 years ago'* which implies that some semblance of the Riding could be seen as late as in the 1890s or 1880s.

*The Jubilee mentioned in the passage above marked the 25th regnal year of King George V and Queen Mary; the event is commemorated in Bodmin by Jubilee Terrace, the corporate housing on the northern side of Dunmere Road.

*The writer obviously had little appetite for the Riding as described to him; but, thanks to his recording one 'unsavoury' aspect, we have that delicious glimpse of the drum disappearing down Chapel Lane - doubtless, hardly missed by the very merry Riding bandsmen!

1939

GUARDIAN ARTICLE, March 30, page 8, " 'Q' Talks Of Yesterday & Today".

> *"Sir Arthur spoke of the Bodmin Riding and said with amusement that he had recently been asked by a correspondent whether the tune was played when the bones of St. Petroc were brought back to Bodmin in the Casket! Asked if he remembered the Riding, he said he did, indeed. They, the general company who danced to the tune, would start off at the bottom of the town calling at every pub as they danced their way up through the street. By the time they got to the Garland Ox, it would seem that they were in no mood to go much further. But even so, the final resting place was the Borough Arms. Sir Arthur was much amused as he recalled these goings on and smiled gleefully as he pictured again this old custom which has now died out."*

NOTES

*Known by his pen-name 'Q', Sir Arthur Quiller-Couch was the Bodmin-born novelist, poet, essayist and scholar: Dr. Couch's son. Born in Pool Street and baptised at Bodmin parish church, he was educated at the school of the Misses Lutman near his later home in Fore Street; and then progressed to Newton Abbot College in Devon, Clifton College in Bristol and Trinity College, Oxford where he eventually became a don. He was knighted in 1910; and became Professor of English Literature at Cambridge two years later.

*At the time of the interview above, which took place five years before his death, he was 76 years of age and living at 'The Haven' in Fowey. He had settled in that town in 1892 and married into a local family.

*The Ridings of his remembrance must have taken place at the end of the 1860s or beginning of the 1870s; the recollections above are similar to those of W.J.P. Burton but, from Quiller-Couch, we learn that the destination was Dunmere.

*The episode concerning St. Petroc, which so amused 'Q', is illustrative of the way in which the mere mention by his father, that some considered the Riding commemorative of the restitution of Petroc's relics, had been accepted and handed down as fact for decades. (See the 4th note under the date 1803-1816)

*The passage above shows that the Riding was certainly still in existence when Dr. Couch wrote in 1864 but that the form it took by that time, as described by his son here, was unacceptable to him as the Riding proper.

*This completes the eye-witness accounts or recollections of those living at the time when the Riding was still an annual event. There are many other writers who could be quoted - we have already mentioned several including Redding under the date 1602 and Polsue, Maclean, Wilkinson and Courtney under the date 1864 - but they tend to have followed our main reporters of the festival or merely to have commented upon various interpretations. Mention should however be made of Mr. C. Skinner, whose recollections went back to 1866 and the Riding when, as a nonagenarian member of the Bodmin 'Over 65s' Club, he was featured in the Guardian during the early 1950s.

REVIVAL 1974

As may be gathered from the foregoing, several attempts have been made to revive the Riding during the present century. Among similar suggestions since 1935 have been those of Mr. G.W.F. Ellis in the late 1940s, the present writer as Chamber of Commerce secretary in 1967, and Mr. J.H. Pethybridge as newly elected and last borough mayor in 1973. The last named's hope of seeing the Riding revived was taken in earnest by the events secretary to the Bodmin committee of the Save The Children Fund, Mrs. Megan Perry, who set in motion a feasibility study. As her committee was already preparing a restoration of the Bodmin Horse Show - and it was suspected that that event had originated as part of the Riding sports - it was decided to extend the show's scope to embrace a Riding and that the combined event be held as nearly as possible to the traditional July date.

Meanwhile, however, and because 1974 was to be the year of local government reorganisation, the then town clerk had considered how the occasion of the change-over from Bodmin Borough to Bodmin Town Council could most suitably be marked. Having come to the conclusion that a revival of the town's festival could be appropriate, he had approached the Rotary Club as its President and gained members' agreement to organise the event. It was therefore finally arranged that, while the Save The Children Fund committee continued with its preparations for a Horse Show in July, the Rotarians would produce the Riding to coincide with the election of the first town mayor in May.

So, following the election at mid-day in the guildhall and subsequent reception in the public rooms of Mr. Councillor W.J.H. Burden on Tuesday, May 21, a civic service took place in the parish church of St. Petroc that evening with the twofold purpose of marking a new chapter in the municipal history of Bodmin and of commencing a revival of the town's ancient feast. On the evening of the following day, Wednesday, May 22, participants and entrants assembled on the south bank of the Priory Park Football Field to be marshalled and judged respectively. Then, at about 6.30 p.m., the procession formed up and moved westward towards the Mount Folly Square.

Just before it reached that point, the door of Shire House opened and the town mayor and mayoress accompanied by Mr. Councillor I.S. MacWatt, deputy town mayor, and Mr. E. Rowe, the new town clerk, descended the steps and crossed the road to take up a position on the traffic island at the top of Turf Street escorted by Mr. A. Nicholas, town crier, and Messrs. C. Trust and W. Rowe, sergeants-at-mace. There, the town mayor and his deputy received the stewards of the Riding, Messrs. I. Whiting and J. Sebbage, President and 1st Vice President of the Rotary Club respectively, presenting them in turn with a floral pole and garland which had been created for and in the tradition of the occasion by Mr. and Mrs. H.J. Vine. Then, the stewards of the Riding ale, Mr. and Mrs. A. Haynes of Shire House, dispensed the liquor from Mr. J. Lauri-Smith's hand-carved leathern bombard into black-jacks for the tasting ceremonial. As the latter ended, an 1882 landau from the Camborne Carriage Museum was drawn alongside by Mr. and Miss Gotts, the coachman and groom; and the town mayor, town mayoress, deputy town mayor and town clerk took their places in the open carriage as a detachment of Cornishmen, in Peninsular War uniforms, from the Light Infantry formed an escort.

With Mr. R.J. Lobb of Norton riding in front of the coach and sergeants-at-mace, town crier and Riding stewards walking behind it, the first part of the procession moved through the crowded Mount Folly Square, around the Turret Clock, and into Honey Street. Next marched the Bodmin Town Band playing the Riding tune; and, behind it, danced children from the County Junior School under the direction of Mrs. Joan Hore, St. Petroc's Anglican Junior School under Miss Dorothy Barrett, and St. Mary's Roman Catholic Junior School under Mrs. Shirley Chapman.

Following the participants came some 50 entrants of the six competitive classes representing trades and professions in pre-1900 costumes. Walkers included a team of balloonists, a match-seller, a band of peasant labourers, and a late-19th century D.C.L.I. soldier in walking-out uniform (prizes: Senior Aircraftsman Hilton, Mr. Ted Burgess, and 42 Squadron R.A.F. St. Mawgan). Among the junior Riding entrants were an 1820s milkmaid, an 18th century infantryman, and a youngster in topper and tails (prizes: Ellen Whiting, Julian Whiting and Finion Green), while senior riders included a besmirched chimneysweep and a plumed, princely figure (prizes: Richard Bowden and Geoffrey Gotts). Characters from the Puritan, Stuart and Napoleonic periods rode amongst the adult entrants (prizes: Mr. Franklin Cory, Mrs. J. Richards, and Flt. Sgt. Nicholson).

Next came the decorated horses, their brasses catching the sunlight and tinkling their approach, Duke and Prince respectively from English China Clays taking the class prizes. And, finally, the horse-drawn vehicles moved sedately between the ranks of onlookers, Fiona Russell taking not only the first prize for this class but the Riding cup for the best entrant, while the St. Austell Driving Club gained the second class prize. Continuing from Honey Street, the Riding procession passed through the Church Square and into the Dennison Road and members of the Rotary Club kept pace as they collected money in aid of charity from those who lined the route.

As all good folk festivals should not be without incident, Bodmin's kept up the reputation that evening, the mayoral carriage setting the example. Firstly, one of its wheels struck a young onlooker as it left the Priory Park and members on duty from the St.John Ambulance Brigade came swiftly and successfully to her rescue;secondly, as it drew level with the Dennison Road 'bus shelter, its horse obeyed nature rather than decorum with the result that the procession, having come to a halt while the animal acted upon impulse, had to divide into two ranks as the carriage moved off behind its unburdened beast. Even then all was apparently not well for, thirdly, as the horse reached the Burnard's Lane gate into the former railway station it reared and the last the present writer saw of the mayoral party on the ring road was the jolting rear of its carriage as it sped around the corner towards the Town Wall. Nevertheless, the leading mount, sergeants-at-mace, town crier and Riding stewards walked on regardless while the rest of the parade played, danced, walked and rode oblivious to the drama in front!

The incline up to the Town Wall proved too much for the boisterous coach-puller, however, so Mr. Mayor and his companions relieved him of their weight and walked to the top. Nearby, in the best tradition of the Riding, refreshment was taken at the Barley Sheaf. Then, in correct order of procession and with this fortification, the Riding proceeded down Fore Street casting long shadows before it as the pale sun was by that time low in the sky. After another tasting, this time at the Queen's Head, the procession re-crossed the Mount Folly Square and disbanded where it had all begun - in the Priory.

Customary sports followed, the Rotary Club's donkey derby and tug-o-war match which had been held annually since 1972 being the events of the evening on the Football Field. Five pulls took place between the six races and the team from Lezant eventually won the tug-o-war contest. Over £200 had been raised for charity. Bodmin Riding had at last been revived and, true to form, had attracted participants from as far away as Camborne and Lezant. Perhaps a century had elapsed between this revival and the last full-scale festival which ended in the Borough Arms at Dunmere. Now Bodmin understood why its forebears had kept up the Riding for at least five hundred years until then. Here's to the next half-millennium!

*Please study the appendices at the end of this book in order to compare your comments and conclusions with those of the authoress in the intervening pages.

comments and conclusions

comments and conclusions

Having reviewed as much as has been discovered about the Bodmin Riding custom, we now have to draw some conclusions as to its origin and meaning.

Summary: The Riding's Development:

In the 15th century, five trades guilds were connected with a jaunt held on Riding Day; some of its proceeds were donated towards the parish church rebuilding fund and the latter's receiver spent 55p at the event. In the 16th century, guilds associated with the Riding were connected with the erection of Bery Tower, skilled shoemakers were obliged by order of the mayor and their masters to attend church during the Riding; and sports, including a mock court, took place at Halgavor. In the 17th century, the heir to the throne so enjoyed a mid-July carnival - apparently at Halgavor - that he became a brother of its organising society; the mayor presented wine to members of the gentry at the Riding; and, on the two Mondays after July 7, a great concourse of people rode to church with a garlanded timber and then proceeded in trades groups to Bodmin downs where sports included running and riding for silver prizes.

The century up to 1700 brought about changes in the Riding's procedure, probably as the result of civil war and a lapse in observance during that period. Further variations are discernible in the 18th century: in the first half, while Halgavor sports continued to attract thousands of people and Mr. Robartes donated a venison to the Riding, there was no church service. When the last-named was restored, some time in the second half of the century, it took place on the Sunday instead of the Monday nearest to July 7, the latter day being reserved for a procession of musicians and trades groups to the Priory, where a previously deposited garland and a decorated pole were received, and sports sponsored by gentlemen of the locality.

BODMIN RIDING

Opinions seem to agree that, during the first quarter of the
19th century, the festival declined and only the ordinary people rode
into the countryside (to pay respects to St. Benet's and other places)
and then presented garlands at the Priory on the Monday after July 7;
but accounts differ as to whether or not the Halgavor carnival continued.
However, in 1824 - the year in which horse racing, which had become a
separate event at some time after 1700, was discontinued - a revival of
the Riding was organised for Monday, Tuesday and Wednesday, the 19th
20th and 21st of July with a marked emphasis on the sports which included wrestling and ringing. And those past middle-age in 1864 could
also remember a three-day celebration, beginning on the Sunday after
July 7, when young men carried Riding ale around the town in baskets.
This, brewed the previous October and already enjoyed at a minor
merry-making about Whitsuntide, they invited householders to taste in
return for contributions towards the festivities, after the customary
crier's salutation and while the drum and fife band played the Riding
tune. The following day, a mounted procession collected two garlanded
staves from the Priory en route to two-day sports at Town End which
included wrestling, running and jumping in sacks.

Meanwhile and although an actual 'riding' seems to have been
omitted, events during the 1840s and 1850s appear to have re-won
the patronage of principal inhabitants, one at least actually leading the
evening flora dance. The Riding, then, commenced at 4 a.m. on the
second Monday in July when the Teetotal Drum & Fife Band led a procession from the Turret Clock, up Fore Street and through Bore and
Pool Streets, participants being regaled with free drinks at the inns along
the way. At 10 a.m., the corporation proceeded to church; and, in the
afternoon, sports on the Beacon amid booths and stalls included wrestling in the ring, there being also horse events on the Racecourse before
General Gilbert's death in 1853. Celebrations continued throughout
the week and inhabitants were permitted to brew their own beer for
the occasion. Such procedure seems to have obtained in the late 1860s
and 1870s, possibly continuing into the 1880s; but, as the Riding had
degenerated by the last years into a mere dance to the tune from inn to
inn until Dunmere was reached, the authorities apparently suppressed
its annual observance so that it was scarcely remembered by 1903.

Possible Interpretations:

In our reviews of the various records which have enabled us to
reconstruct the development of the Riding, we have considered some
interpretations that have been put forward during the past two centuries
together with new ideas. It now remains for us to clarify a few points.
Mock officials and courts have been thought of as survivals from Celtic

or even pre-Celtic times, such ancient procedures being tolerated by subsequent conquerors during traditional festivals: and it is noticeable that the mock elections mentioned in Appendix 4 took place in Cornish areas generally during parish feasts or fairs, most of the remainder occurring on official mayor-choosing days. It therefore appears feasible that Bodmin's Halgavor Court Sports, held in the middle of July at least by the 18th century, would fall into the general category. As we have found little reason to believe other than that Cox's account of Prince Charles's attendance is credible, his use of the words 'brother' and 'society' directly links the Halgavor proceedings with those of the Riding.

From Lhuyd's account, it is apparent that the Riding extended into the middle of July, the season of the Halgavor Sports; and, as we have shown under the date 1820, it is probable that the site of both the Riding sports and of the latter was to the south west of what is now called The Beacon, originally part of Halgavor Moor and then designated Bodmin Downs. If there is now the possibility of the Riding and Halgavor Sports being two parts of one festival, the idea that that celebration could have been Bodmin's equivalent of a Cornish parish feast presents itself. And 'feast' is, of course, the description used by the earliest reporter of the Riding - Lhuyd.

If many writers of the past would disagree with our linking the Riding with Halgavor Court Sports, it is because Carew described the latter as though it was an occasional prank and without mentioning the former. It might be reiterated, however, that Carew omitted mention of Padstow's 'Obby 'Oss although we know it existed; and it could be accepted that Halgavor Court occasionally sat at random, rather as the Riding sometimes took place at Rogationtide in place of the bounds' beating. It should also be noticed that, although we know of so many Cornish mock mayors, the Halgavor mayor was Carew's example; and despite the fame of Bodmin's Riding, only the similar procession at Lostwithiel was recorded by Carew.

Mock mayors and judge apart, one of the main differences between Lostwithiel's Riding and the events at Bodmin and Liskeard would appear to be that, whereas the procession at the first town accompanied a personage or his representative, the riders in the other two towns paraded with decorated poles. Herein could lie a clue to the ages of the three customs: the personage represented at Lostwithiel was probably one of the Earls or Dukes of Cornwall, which would make that town's procession of medieval origin; but the poles at Liskeard and Bodmin could indicate a much earlier derivation. In this respect, the descriptions in Appendix 4 of 'riding effigies' are relevant for they give us a glimpse of what might once have been witnessed during parish feasts. If we cross the Channel to Brittany and examine that region's annual parish festivals called Pardons, it will be found that effigies and/

or relics of the saintly patrons are paraded on poles. Were it not for
the Reformation, similar procedure might have continued in Cornwall:
the riotous events which ended in court at St. Dominick and Redruth in
the 19th century possibly being diminished survivals, or folk judgements
in burlesque, of such.

Our return to the possibility of the Riding's having been the
equivalent of a parish feast poses the question as to whose effigy was
originally carried on the Bodmin pole, if that was its purpose. There is
always, of course, Thomas Becket to consider in view of the coincidence
of his translation and the Riding's season. But as, other than that, there
is little to suggest his being regarded as a patron of Bodmin, the most
likely candidates would be Guron, Petroc, possibly Athelstan, and King
Edgar. As we have shown under the date 1903 and in Appendix 1, our
inclination is towards the last-named for, apart from Lostwithiel's mock
prince and Bath's mock king, there is at least one other parallel which
ought to be cited. The occasion in 1199 when Henry II's son, John
Lackland, granted the vintners of St. Emilion guild membership is,
almost eight centuries later, still commemorated by a May festival in
the Gironde departement of South West France. As we know that Edgar
was a patron of St. Petroc's Priory and that clerics could be guildsmen;
and, as guildsmen were connected with the Riding which fell on or near
Edgar's Day, it is difficult to decide other than that King Edgar's patronage was commemorated by a town whose official crest portrays a regal
figure. And Edgar could also be relevant in the Liskeard context as we
note in Appendix 3. One difference, which might be pointed out between the customs of St. Emilion and Bath and those of Lostwithiel,
Liskeard and Bodmin, could be that the last three towns have forgotten
the names of their patrons!

Features of the Riding, other than those already mentioned,
may have developed later when the gentry, unable to travel abroad during the French Revolutionary and Napoleonic Wars, amused themselves
at home by encouraging local customs. This would certainly explain
the visits to mansions, such as the Priory and St. Benet's, as courtesy
gestures to sponsors of the Riding and sports; the music, if it is also of
that period, could have been introduced by French officers on parole in
the town. The flora or furry dance, so dear to the Cornish, was probably originally a spontaneous performance general to any celebration
rather than something of peculiar significance to the Riding. But it is
more difficult to determine whether the ale ceremonial, crier's salute
and 4 a.m. knock-up were of great antiquity or of fairly recent origin.
A 4 a.m. apprentices' bell was rung in Bodmin, as well as the extant
curfew, from the 17th century at least; and, as an early borough,
Bodmin would have had a town crier or beadle from medieval times
and that officer has played a customary role in the bounds' beating
tradition. Moreover, in the middle ages, festivals were actually
known as 'ales' when they were held for the collection of dues, town or

guild rates usually being settled at scot-ales and parish rates at church-ales. We might therefore say that, as the Riding was a town event including the mayor and principal tradesmen, the borough's annual feast began at the hour when apprentices were called to work and that householders paid their dues in return for Riding ale before attending customary celebrations. In the absence of firm proof, however, this - and perhaps all of our comments and conclusions - should remain within the realm of speculation.

The Riding Compared With Other Customs

Compared with other folk festivals still observed in Cornwall - Padstow's 'Obby 'Oss, St. Ives' and St. Columb's Hurling, and Helston's Furry Dance - the Bodmin Riding appears to have the earliest documentation by several decades. But it is held later in the year: Hurling being at Springtime and the 'Obby 'Oss and Furry welcoming Summer; however, the other three customs - like the Riding - could be and were held at different times and at places other than those with which we have come to associate them, even beyond our shores.

Certain folk elements seem common to them all. Each has a distinctive tune, yet their underlying rhythms have a haunting similarity; each includes fertility symbolism: flowers and the traditional (sycamore) greenery being brought in from the countryside for the Riding, 'Obby 'Oss and Furry, and the (originally golden) ball of the Hurling being thrown up - possibly to represent the sun's rise in the sky at Springtime and being passed around for good luck. During the observance of all there is a perambulation of the town whether by riding, playing or dancing; and certain customary visits are made. They also have an apparently inevitable association with alcohol: Helston's Hal-an-Tow being discontinued until 1930 due to the 'drunken revels' it produced, Bodmin's Riding suffering a similar fate until 1974, the home of Padstow's Old 'Oss being an inn, and St. Columb's (now silver) ball being ceremonially immersed at the inns so that hurlers and onlookers might enjoy 'silver beer' at the end of the game.

Although, particularly at St. Ives, Hurling has religious and civic connections, actual attendance at church and involvement of the local authority are limited to the Furry and the Riding. As for town decorations of bunting and greenery, garlanded and beribboned dancers, and an early-morning start, these are common to the customs with pre-feast activities: the Riding and its minor Whitsuntide merrymaking, the Furry and its May Day playing of the tune, and the 'Obby 'Oss with its late-night song rehearsals.

ENVOI

Some tentative conclusions, with regard to the meaning of certain aspects of the Riding at given times, may now have been reached. But what of its origins?

If other traditions have been said to be as old as man himself, there is every likelihood that the Riding's beginnings are enveloped in the mists of unrecorded antiquity. For instance, its midsummer season and flowers suggest a prehistoric ceremony; and its equestrian events could link it with the pagan games witnessed by St. Samson in the 5th/6th century. On the other hand, the suspected connection with bounds' beating might point to a slightly later origin parallel with the Breton tromenie or circuit of the sanctuary of a Celtic missionary.

If Polwhele was right in thinking that pagan customs were adopted and adapted for Christian purposes, the Riding could have been part of all of these as it developed. By the later dark ages, it may well have come within the realm of the Saxon borough bounds' beating, the Scottish perambulation of lands won in battle, or even the Scandinavian thriding - associations which might be established by an investigation beyond the scope of this small work.

The Riding's earliest recorded phase in the mid-15th century shows it to have been very much an affair of the guilds. And we have reviewed in this book the ways in which it has changed since then so as to bear little resemblance even to that.

Only one thing can be said of Bodmin Riding with certainty: Bodmin loved it, whatever its origin or meaning, and cherished it as a town event long after most other places had abandoned similar observances. That, at least, is worth recording in this way and attempting to discover why.

Hal-an-tow, mentioned on page 78, was originally a parish bounds' beat including an early-morning knock-up, drum music, house-to-house collections, flowers and greenery from the countryside, and a pole ride and river dunking for anyone caught working.

For descriptions of other customs mentioned

"Padstow's 'Obby 'Oss", D R Rawe, Lodenek Press, 1971

"Hurling At St Columb", A L Rabey, Lodenek Press, 1972

"The Helston Furry Dance", The Association, Helston Town Hall.

APPENDIX ONE

BATH'S MOCK KING - according to John Leland, 'Itinerary', 1534-1543 (Royal Institution Of Cornwall Museum, Truro).

"King Edgar was crowned with much joy and honour at St. Peter's in Bath, whereupon he bare great zeal to the town and gave very great franchises and privileges unto it. In knowledge whereof they pray in all their ceremonies for the soul of King Edgar.

And at Whitsuntide, at the which time men say that Edgar there was crowned, there is a king elected at Bath every year of the townsmen in the joyful remembrance of King Edgar and the privileges given to the town by him. This (mock) king is fested, and his adherants, by the richest men of the town."

NOTES

*John Leland was born in London in about 1506 and was known as 'junior' as his elder brother was of the same name. In 1533 he became King Henry VIII's antiquary and undertook to record items of interest and value during the Reformation, his tour lasting from 1534 to 1543.

*King Edgar was crowned at Bath at the age of 29, the ceremony in the Saxon abbey on Whitsunday, May 11, 973 providing the model for subsequent coronation services in many respects. Born in the year his mother died, 944, he had been chosen King of the English when barely 16 in October of 959 upon the death of his brother, King Edwy. Despite his kindly attitude toward Danish subjects making him unpopular in some quarters and scandal surrounding the births of his first two children early in his reign, the people took to him. It is said that rulers of the Isles, the Scots, the Welsh and of Cumberland declared their vassalage after his coronation by rowing his boat at the head of a great flotilla. Influenced and assisted by Dunstan, Archbishop of Canterbury, Edgar became a zealous patron of monks and founder and reformer of monasteries. His peaceful and constructive reign came to an untimely end when he died on July 8, 975 aged only 31. Buried at Glastonbury, his body was translated in 1052 to a shrine above the altar of the abbey church where he was revered as a saint.

*The passage above is an indication of the impact his coronation had upon Bath as its anniversary was kept up even six centuries later. The *'richest men'* who did so obviously benefited from the resultant prestige and were equivalent to the freeholders at Lostwithiel and guildsmen of Bodmin who were prominent in the Ridings. In fact, it is evident that the customs of Lostwithiel and Liskeard had some connection with the Crown; and there is reason to believe similarly of Bodmin's.

*As the official seal of Bodmin depicts a crowned figure seated in state and holding a sceptre, it is not too much to assume that the town's feast was in honour of a royal patron. And, as the seal was authorised by the borough's Elizabethan charter of 1562/3 and registered at the Herald's Visitation in 1620 (certificate: Harley Ms. 1164, 72; British Library Manuscripts Department, London), the candidate should be prior to 1558. In fact Leland reported that a King was regarded as patron of Bodmin in the 1530s and he was given to understand that it was Athelstan (see under the date 1903). There seems little to support this, however, as the Exeter charter showing Athelstan's grant of Newton manor to St. Petroc's Priory is considered 'dubious' (G.H. Doble, "Petroc", 3rd ed. 1938) and the gift is more likely to have been Edred's as confirmed by Henry III in 1272. But beyond all doubt are the facts that Edgar ordered the shrine of Petroc to be gilded in 963; and slaves were freed in that king's name before the Conquest at Petroc's foundations (Doble; and Bodmin Gospels: British Museum Ancient Manuscripts Dpt., Add. Ms. 9381) Even as late as the 16th century, Edgar's emblem was used by a Bodmin prior. If Bath could commemorate that king with an annual pageant, there is no reason to believe that Bodmin could not.

APPENDIX TWO

LOSTWITHIEL RIDING & MOCK PRINCE - according to Richard Carew, "Survey of Cornwall", 1602; Book Two, Powder Hundred -

"Upon little Easter Sunday the freeholders of the town and manor, by themselves or their deputies, did there assemble: amongst whom, one (as it fell to his lot by turn) bravely apparelled, gallantly mounted, with a crown on his head, a sceptre in his hand, a sword borne before him, and dutifully attended by all the rest on horseback, rode through the principal street to the church; there the curate in his best beseen solemnly received him at the churchyard stile and conducted him to hear divine service; after which he repaired with the same pomp to a house *foreprovided for that purpose, made a feast to his attendants, kept the table's end himself, and was served with kneeling, assay, and all other rights due to the estate of a prince: with which dinner the ceremony ended, and every man returned home again. The pedigree of this usage is derived from so many descents of ages that the cause and author* outreach remembrance: howbeit, these circumstances offer *a conjecture that it should betoken the royalties appertaining to the honour of Cornwall.*
This solemn custom was in times past here yearly observed, and only of late days discontinued."

NOTES

* *"Little Easter Sunday"* is Low Sunday, the Sunday after Easter Sunday.
*By virtue of their being at the head of the Fowey estuary and within the vicinity of medievel tin workings, Restormel Castle and Lostwithiel Borough were acquired by Henry III's brother Richard, Earl of Cornwall, shortly before his death in 1272. It is probable that both he and his son, Edmund, Earl of Cornwall, visited the castle and were received by the borough. Certainly the Black Prince, Edward, the first Duke of Cornwall, visited Restormel during the Summer of 1354 and at Easter 1363 according to Charles Henderson ('Essays', Oxford, 1935).
*The *"freeholders of the town and manor"* mentioned above would probably originally have been members of the Merchant Guild which Lostwithiel was granted in 1268/9. It is possible that they escorted the Prince to church and entertained, or were entertained by, him afterwards. This event has the interesting parallel of Bath's mock king yet, at the same time, is reminiscent of Bodmin's Riding.

*As Carew noted, the origin and meaning of the custom had been forgotten. But, while it might be tempting to connect the word *'assay'* with Cornish tin, to purchase which the Earls and Dukes had the right of first refusal, it does in the context of the passage above mean the act of tasting food or drink before offering it to an exalted personage. Nevertheless, the *'feast'* could well have been the equivalent of a scot-ale when medieval dues were collected.

*The *'sword borne before him'* brings to mind the staves carried at Bodmin and Liskeard. But, as there is no mention of its being decorated, we may take it that it was a sword of state, symbolic of authority.

*The present writer had the privilege of providing extracts from this appendix for a revival of the pageant which took place at Restormel on August 24, 1974. It may be noticed that we have referred to the Lostwithiel and Liskeard processions as *Ridings* although they are not described as such in their records. This liberty has been taken in order to avoid the repeated use of inverted commas.

APPENDIX THREE

LISKEARD RIDING & MOCK JUDGE - according to 'The History Of The Borough Of Liskeard' by John Allen, 1856; edited and revised by W.H. Paynter, 1967; pages 139-140.

"The great period of amusement and merriment at Liskeard was the week of Whitsuntide - possibly the relic of an old parish feast, celebrated at that season. According to an ancient record of Exeter Cathedral 'on the 11 June, 1381, Bishop Brantyngham transferred the parish wake of Liskeard from the eve of St. Bartholomew (Aug. 23) to the translation of St. Martin's relics which, according to Bishop Grandisson, took place in June 1001'. This may account for the long continued celebration of games at Whitsuntide, which fell in this or the preceding month.

From time immemorial till about 1810 the publicans, aided by the contributions of other individuals, invariably held at Whitsuntide certain gymnastic games such as wrestling, cudgel-playing, gingling, jumping in sacks, donkey racing etc. for a variety of prizes: a purse of guineas, gold lace and plain hats etc. These were hoisted on poles and drummed round the town, on several market days and on the fair day before the games, by a procession of ragged boys who halted at the doors of public houses and got up a cheer when, as a matter of course, a jug of beer or cider was brought out to them. On Monday when the games began, a pretended judge - generally an old man selected for his wit, drollery and love of drink - went in procession with music round the town, two pages holding up his train, attended by other officials, a sheriff's troop and javelin men: the whole consisting of about thirty on horseback decorated with ribbons and flowers carrying a painted staff so adorned and collecting a concourse of spectators and followers.

On Tuesday, the innkeepers furnished gratuitously a carriage for his lordship, the pages mounted behind. On the last day, Wednesday, after another circuit of the town a sort of mock criminal court was held. The game field or frolic green in Lamellion Street was the place of judicature where the delinquents - some low depraved characters - would be put upon their trial for alleged or real offences, convicted and sentenced to the performance of something of a disagreeable and facetious nature for punishment; a dance also took place on the grass. To complete the affair, a couple of rough, reckless fellows -

*one clad as a female and armed with a ladle and the other
with a broom - designated John and Joan led the last
procession and belaboured those within their reach
exhibiting disgusting grimaces of gross intemperance.
Strange though it may seem, the observance of Whitsuntide
appeared to meet with general approval, the town being
almost deserted on the occasion and many of most classes
giving encouragement by subscribing and being present
at part of the games at least.*

NOTES

*Above is a mid-19th century account, roughly contemporary with
Couch's article on Bodmin's event, of a festival in Liskeard remarkably
like the Riding. The prizes, reminiscent of those offered at the 1824
revival in Bodmin, having been drummed around Liskeard on poles to
advertise forthcoming festivities and the liquor having already flowed,
events proper began on a Monday as at Bodmin. That first day included
a mock judicial procession complete with sheriff's troop and javelin men
and, as in Bodmin, the carrying of a beribboned and garlanded staff.
Another procession took place on the Tuesday, the second day of the
presumably continuous sports; and two more processions were held on
the Wednesday, one before and the other after the mock court and
dance.

*As the Riding above is said to have been discontinued by about 1810,
we may take it that the description is a composite of recollections of
several occasions during the late 18th century or early 19th. There is,
of course, always the danger that Allen may have portrayed an 'ideal'
festival just as we suspect Dr. Couch to have dealt with Bodmin's
Riding; irrespective of this possibility and in the absence of other mat-
erial, we must gather those impressions we may and an inevitable
conclusion is that Liskeard's events were almost identical in many respects to Bodmin's.

*The account is at too late a date for firm decisions as to the event's
probable origin and meaning to be taken, the words *'ragged boys'*,
'rough, reckless fellows' and *'publicans'* indicating a festival already,
perhaps, in decline. However, from the opening paragraph, it may be
seen that Allen suspected there to have been religious associations. In
fact, it has been thought that Liskeard had some connection with St.
Petroc's Priory before the Conquest by virtue of the Saint's bell having
been taken there from Bodmin for a slave freedom ceremony. This
possibility would reintroduce the question of King Edgar, the esteemed
patron of the monastery; certainly, were both Liskeard and Bodmin
Ridings connected with a festival in his honour, it would explain their
extraordinary similarities. The Whitsuntide season of Liskeard's Riding

would in no way refute such a theory, even although Edgar's Day was July 8, as the town's feast date is stated to have been altered at least once; and, in any case, Bodmin is supposed to have celebrated also around Whitsuntide: the season of Edgar's coronation.

*Liskeard's Riding, as described above, seems to have been adopted by local publicans who, by that period, had become its patrons, although the final statement, regarding *'many of most classes'* subscribing and attending, is reminiscent of W.R. Gilbert's closing remarks concerning presents from and attendance of *'gentlemen of the neighbourhood'*. The inn-keepers' close association with Liskeard's Riding, however, is of interest in as far as we suspect Bodmin's ale ceremonial to have been introduced or developed by local publicans.

*During the pre-feast activities, which seem common to most customs, we are told that the prizes were *'drummed'* around the town; and there is a later mention of dancing on the green but no special music seems to have been recorded for Liskeard's Riding. The antics of *'John and Joan'*, as they led the final procession, would seem to compare with those expected of the Bodmin characters who led the evening flora dance; but worthy of more than passing interest are John and Joan themselves: one being a man dressed as a woman and the other carrying a broom. Such devices could connect this part of the proceedings with the Morris Dances, in which it was customary for a 'female' to accompany the hobby horse, and it seems possible that the broom might have been a horse-head on a stick. (But see St. Dominick, page 89)

*Were there any doubt that the Halgavor Court was once part of Bodmin's Riding after a review of the passage above, it would be surprising; the judicial element in Liskeard's Riding may be puzzling, however, for while it might have been a burlesque of the judge's arrival in Launceston at Springtime and in Bodmin during the Summer before 1836, Liskeard seems never to have accommodated the Assizes. But it was, of course, an Earldom and later Duchy of Cornwall borough, being chartered and granted a Merchant Guild in 1240 by Earl Richard - who built a fortified manor-house, called the castle, in the town - and being the venue of some Duchy audits. And another association enjoyed by Liskeard, in common with Bodmin in early medieval times, was with the tin trade as a Coinage Town. Therefore, with borough, guild, Stannary and Duchy courts, Liskeard must have witnessed considerable pageantry in the middle ages, some remnants of which are discernible in the passage above.

APPENDIX FOUR

MOCK MAYORS & RIDINGS

* A.K. Hamilton Jenkin, 'Cornish Homes & Customs,' 1934 (reprint by David & Charles in composite form entitled 'Cornwall & Its People' 1970, pages 470-471) - the following events are cited:

Launceston mock Mayor of the Pig Market elected on mayor choosing day and festivities connected with the New Inn.

Chacewater mock mayor elected until World War One, connected with ale.

Lanner mock mayor elected on Boxing Day, connected with a drum-and-fife band, a donkey-riding, and a Cuckle's Court and ale in the Miners Arms.

Constantine mock mayor until 1857, elected on the Wednesday after the parish feast and dragged in a cart from the Queens Arms and toppled into a river.

Halsetown (St. Ives), although a new village in 1830, adopted the custom of electing a mock mayor, on mayor choosing day; banquet in the inn.

St. Neot, Pelynt, Budock, Peace, Illogan, Four Lanes, Stithians and *Crowlas* all elected mock mayors: usually in parish feast week, connected with ale, and often coming to some ignominious end in fun.

Such customs were widespread across Europe and parallel events may be traced even to India.

*M.A. Courtney, 'Cornish Feasts & Folklore', 1886/7 (reprint by E.P. Publishing Ltd. 1973, pages 27, 37, 45-46) - the following events are cited:

St. John's, Helston, mock mayor, still elected 1886.

Buryan mock mayor, still elected 1886.

Penzance mock Mayor of the Quay until about 1876.

Lostwithiel mock mayor elected by torchlight in the presence of almost 1,000 people on October 10, 1884.

St. Germans mock mayor elected at a beer house, May 29, as part of May Fair celebrations; paraded in a cart; Fair Ale drunk.

Polperro mock mayor elected during St. Peter's Fair in mid-July; he appointed his officers; paraded in a cart from inn to inn and finally into the sea.

Penryn mock mayor elected, as part of autumnal Nutting Day festivities, by journeymen tailors who chose him from Mylor. Preceded by torch bearers and sergeants-at-mace, he was chaired into Penryn where the band played him from inn to inn. Dinner at an inn, a bonfire and fireworks ended the day.

***John Burton, 'Bygone Days In Bodmin', The Guardian newspaper, March 24, 1905, page 4 (Bodmin Reference Library) -**

'After the ST. LAWRENCE roast goose fair in October was over . . . the mayor choosing took place. The candidate first found drunk was pitched into a wheelbarrow, driven down the village and, when on the bridge, was thrown into the river and duly elected Mayor of St. Lawrence.'

***E.G. Martyn, 'In Reminiscent Mood', The Guardian Newspaper, January 28, 1937, page 7 (Bodmin Reference Library) -**

Speaking to the Wadebridge Old Cornwall Society, Mr. Martyn said that the chief local fair *'was held on ST. BREOCK Feast Day, October 10, and was noted for much carousing. The first man found drunk was driven around in a barrow and made mayor for the ensuing year.'*

***Mr. L.E. Long - to whom we are indebted for many references in this appendix - also cites the following:**

Lanivet is known to have elected a mock mayor.

Quintrell Downs inn was connected with a local personality's being dubbed 'The Mayor of Quint' until fairly recently.

***West Briton newspaper, February 8, 1870 (Cornwall Museum, Truro) -**

At the trial of eight men *'summoned for congregating on the highway in the parish of ST. DOMINICK . . . P.C. Hugo stated that on the night in question he was about a mile from the village when he heard a great noise proceeding from the direction of St. Dominick. On going further he heard guns firing and people shouting and on arriving at Ashton he met the defendants . . . they had three large effigies, two clothed in male attire and one female, carrying on a pole. There were three or four in front running, the men with the effigies in the middle and a mob running after. The local name is* **"a Riding".**

*West Briton, June 14, 1875 -

'On May 29 last a lot of roughs conceived the notion of disturbing the public peace by blackening their faces and preparing an effigy and burning it in front of the dwelling-house of Thomas Goldsworthy, a quiet and orderly man . . . Complaints were made by several householders of REDRUTH HIGHWAY of the great and continued nuisance and, on the evening of Saturday, Sergeant Soady went to Highway . . . he found the riot still going on in full force, and a man named Richard Verran, landlord of the "Pick & Gad", with blackened face and grotesque dress, leading a donkey upon which was placed a large effigy. He was followed by about 200 people shouting and yelling at the top of their voices . . .' (The local term for such a caper was apparently **'riding effigies').**

APPENDIX FIVE

SCOTTISH COMMON RIDINGS - according to Graham Williams; travel feature entitled 'A Land That Was Once The Home Of Gypsy Kings, You'll Find Magic & Romance In The Borders'; The Sunday Express, London, June 6, 1971

'This minute house - the gypsy palace of Kirk Yetholm in Roxburghshire - was the home of the gypsy kings of Scotland for centuries. Coronations were frequently held there. Gypsies came from all over Britain for the festivities. After my visit to the palace, which has now been restored as a private house, I climbed the high twisting road to a summit in the Cheviots . . . .
The borderland comprises the counties of Berwick, Roxburgh, Selkirk, Peebles and the eastern tip of Dumfries-shire . . . . In Hawick, the largest of the border towns, I watched 50 horsemen - young, old, merchant and professional men alike - ride out of the town to visit the land which the town owns, the cheers of the townsfolk bidding them "safe oot, safe in".
It was rehearsal for what is called Common Riding later this month. All over the borders these Common Ridings will be held to commemorate victory or defeat in ancient battles.'

NOTES

*A.K. Hamilton Jenkin's 'Cornwall & Its People' (David & Charles reprint, 1970) contains an interesting survey of mock elections, on pages 470 and 471, which could have a bearing on the gypsy coronations mentioned above. It seems possible that they have a parallel in Cornish mock elections. (see appendix 4).

*From the account of borderland Common Ridings above, one origin of our beating of the bounds might be apparent; and, at the same time, the suspicion that Cornish Ridings and bounds' beating may have a common origin is strengthened by the passage above about customs in another Celtic area.

*With the passage above was published a photograph of bowler-hatted horsemen, in hill country, riding behind the standard bearer on the leading mount; and the caption stated that the Common Riding at Selkirk was so pictured. The standard being borne aloft in front of the Scottish Riding may have some bearing on the decorated pole similarly carried in the Cornish Ridings.

*In connection with land boundaries, the Old English and Old Norse 'thriding' or riding ought to be noted. This, meaning 'third part', was an administrative unit - intermediate between a shire and a hundred - which had its own court. The geographical term, usually found in areas of Scandinavian incursion, has not been applied in Cornwall; it might, however, be of interest to consider that the three towns in that county which are known to have kept the Riding custom are situated in the area where Vikings are recorded as having been and suspected to have settled by or during the 10th century.

J.B.CROWLE.

APPENDIX SIX

CORNISH CHURCH ALES - according to Richard Carew, 'Survey Of Cornwall', 1602; Book One on Cornwall in general -

"Their feasts are commonly harvest dinners (between Michaelmas and Candlemas), *church-ales, and the solemnizing of their parish church's dedication which they term their saint's feast.*

For the church-ale, two young men of the parish are yearly chosen by their last foregoers to be wardens, who, dividing the task, make collection among the parishioners of whatsoever provision it pleases them voluntarily to bestow. This they employ in brewing, baking and other dainties, against Whitsuntide, upon which holidays the neighbours meet at the church-house and there merrily feed on their own victuals, contributing some petty portion to the stock, which by many smalls grows to a meetly greatness, for there is entertained a kind of emulation between these wardens, who by his graciousness in gathering and good husbandry in expending, can best advance the church's profit. Besides, the neighbour parishes at those times lovingly visit one another and this way frankly spend their money together. The afternoons are consumed in such exercises as old and young folk (having leisure) do accustomably wear out the time withal.

When the feast is ended, the wardens yield in their account to the parishioners, and such money as exceeds the disbursements is laid up in store to defray any extraordinary charges arising in the parish or imposed on them for the good of the country or the prince's service, neither of which commonly gripe so much but that somewhat still remains to cover the purse's bottom."

NOTES

*Carew continued by saying that church-ales had lately been suppressed as licentious; and, discussing the case for retaining them, cited some uses to which their proceeds were put such as defence, the building of bridges, poor relief, highways, and church repair.

*In view of the last, it is strange that, when Bodmin parish church steeple was struck by lightning in December of 1699 and the borough council subsequently met to consider ways of raising money to repair the damage, no mention was made of the Riding if it was, as Dr. Couch maintained, identical to church-ales. The Riding was certainly in existence during this period, as witness the mayoral accounts for 1690/1 and 1706/7 and Lhuyd's description of 1700.

*In Carew's discussion of a defence of church ales, he mentioned their use in *"defraying at an instant such rates and taxes as the magistrate imposes for the country's defence"*. This shows quite clearly that church-ales were a pleasant method of collecting parish rates. The corporation resolution regarding repair of the damaged church, however, stated that *'no church rates have been ever made within our said borough'*. (Cornwall Record Office: B/BOD 245)

*Carew's description above would have been written at about the time when the Shoemakers' Order was issued in 1583. The guild officials then were called *'stewards'*, as in the parish church accounts 1469/72, not *'wardens'*; and, although John Burton mentioned that townsfolk had licence-by-tradition to brew for the Riding, the ale for the latter was traditionally termed Riding Ale, not church-ale. *'Baking'* for the Riding seems no-where recorded although doubtless some kind of re-freshment was available; however, the emphasis on eating during church-ales probably brought about M.A. Courtney's description of them as *'picnics'* which certainly could not be applied to the Riding with the exception of a suspected corporation banquet. The Whitsuntide period of the church-ales does not coincide with the usual time for the Riding; and, although we have shown that a minor Riding connected with the beating of the bounds took place occasionally at Rogationtide - but a fortnight removed from church-ales' time - no mention of a mounted procession appears in the church-ales record. Bodmin Riding would appear to be a quite different event from church-ales; and, while it is true that the Riding Guild donated towards the re-building of the parish church in the fifteenth century, the fact that nothing seemed forth-coming **by right** in 1699/1700 for church repairs seems to show that the Riding Guild was not the organising body responsible for church-ales which raised parish rates. Even if the corporation's statement re-garding the non-payment of church rates applied only, as stated, *'for the repair of the said church'*, the Riding Guilds' contribution to the re-building conflicts with this **and** the known object of church-ales. But, in any case, church-ales were suppressed by 1602 according to Carew whereas the Riding continued until the 1870s.

*Of the three Cornish feasts outlined by Carew, Bodmin Riding seems to identify best with the parish feast. Each parish apparently 'did its own thing' and, from the appendix dealing with Mock Mayors, it is clear that 'ridings', mock officials, ales and sports all featured in these events. There is no reason, however, for us to identify the Riding with any of Carew's feasts as he made no mention of Padstow's 'Obby 'Oss nor Helston's Furry Day and, in that way, he could have overlooked Bodmin's custom. Nevertheless, the facts that Lhuyd termed the Bodmin Riding a 'feast' in 1700 and that Allen suggested that Liskeard Riding was *possibly the relic of an old parish feast* beg our consideration as to whether or not they may have been patronal celebrations.

But it should be borne in mind that, if the parish feast was on the anniversary of *the solemnizing of their parish church's dedication*, the consecration date of Bodmin's rebuilt church - October 4 - does not coincide with the Riding's season. It is possible, however, that the now unknown and original dedication date was nearer the custom's time.

APPENDIX SEVEN

GUILDS & FESTIVALS

Boroughs are thought to have originated as judicial units separate from shires and hundreds. As agriculture gave way to manufacture and trade, Merchant Guilds were formed within boroughs in order that their business could be regulated by the tradesmen concerned. Not all boroughs had such guilds, those known to have had them in Cornwall being Bodmin by 1179, Helston by 1201, Liskeard by 1240, Lostwithiel by 1269, Dunheved-Launceston by 1272, and Grampound by 1332. Guild courts were distinct from borough courts although guild stewards and borough bailiffs tended to be drawn from the same social circle and often served in both; but, whereas women and clerics could not be burgesses, they could belong to guilds.

In the fourteenth and fifteenth centuries, Merchant Guilds gradually split into craft guilds so that, instead of 'chambers of commerce' for all merchants and craftsmen, there were separate 'trades unions'; and, apart from the latter, there were also semi-religious guilds which may be likened to present-day friendly societies. The fifteenth century parish church accounts show that Bodmin had well over forty different guilds, both trade and religious, operating in the town. Borough corporations often utilised guild halls and, when guilds disappeared from towns, their premises remained as the council meeting places.

Fraternities often bore the names of patron saints or of their aldermen; and were expected to be 'in scot and lot' with the burgesses. This meant that, in return for trade monopoly within a borough, they were expected to assist the municipal authority financially. A guild's method of collecting money from its members was to 'drink the guild'. This entailed the holding of a celebration, usually called an 'ale', to which merchants were invited and where they enjoyed dainties, alcohol and sports while guild stewards assessed them and collected their rates.

The original Merchant Guilds were chartered with their boroughs; and often had power, as Bodmin's guild had under a charter from Richard, Earl of Cornwall, to grant a town's liberty to a runaway serf who had hidden within its bounds for *a year and a day*. A licence for such power was payable annually to the monarch and, when in 1179/80 a raid was made on unlicensed guilds of the south western shires, Bodmin burgesses were fined for keeping a guild without royal warrant.

Below are two examples of guild festivals: the Helston one showing why guild members were summoned to church (reference: Bodmin's Shoe-makers' Order, 1583); and the Ipswich example showing the way in which a 'riding' grew out of an original guild festival:

*Helston Shoemakers' Guild Order (Cornwall Museum, Truro: Henderson Ms. 'Ecclesiastical Antiquities', volume one, page 252 a & b) -

"Be it known to all men that we . . . cordwainers and house-holders of Helston and also servants . . . and other principal founders of the Fraternity of the Trinity in the church of St. Michael . . .
Firstly, we order that on Saturday next after the Feast of the Trinity, every brother and sister come to the said church and there to hear dirges that shall be said for the souls of the brothers and sisters of the said fraternity, and on the morn to hear mass that shall be said upon the Trinity Altar and every brother and sister say a psalter of Our Lady for all the lives and the souls that God wills that we should pray for.
And after, in that same day, every brother and sister come to the house where the wardens will assign, and there to eat and drink in worship of the Trinity, and pay our rent: some 12d, some 8d, some 6d, some 4d and thus yearly to be paid for a man and his wife, and better if they may, every man and woman after his devotion."

NOTES

*This is the first rule in an Order containing several more regulations and may well elucidate the Riding rule in Bodmin's Shoemakers' Order.

'Dirges' were usually connected with funeral services, 'dirge-ale' being the drink taken at funerals. In those times before the welfare state, some of the main purposes of a guild were to ensure that its members were helped if they fell into poverty, that they were 'decently' buried and that their souls were prayed for at least annually.

*Regarding the *'Trinity Altar'* - some guilds had altars within the parish church instead of separate halls or chantries.

*The final sentence above clearly shows that food and drink were offered in return for the payment of dues.

*The date of the Helston Guild Order is uncertain: Charles Henderson ('Essays', Oxford, 1935) giving it as 1517; and H.S. Toy ('History Of Helston', Oxford, 1936) suggesting 1459 or some time in the 16th century.

*Ipswich Corpus Christi Guild (full details of which may be found in "The Guild Merchant" by Charles Gross; Oxford, 1890; page 162)

Gross illustrated the way in which the Ipswich Corpus Christi social-religious guild, newly constituted in 1325, originated from the Merchant Guild set up in that place during the reign of John. And, although the ancient functions of the latter had lapsed by the fourteenth century, *its social-religious successor was a quasi-official part of the civic polity'.*
In fact, the main reason for the existence of the re-constituted guild was to organise a yearly procession on Corpus Christi Day. Every burgess was expected to be a member of the guild which was often allowed wine and money by the town-treasury; a guild priest was maintained by the town to sing and pray for guild members; and, while two aldermen or guild masters were answerable to the corporation for the provision of the procession banquet, the borough court issued orders for the observance of the ceremony. The actual Corpus Christi Procession entailed priests and trades companies marching through the town displaying banners and pageants and it was followed by a feast with wine and fiddlers. Gross also cited Lynn's Merchant Guild which was transformed into the Holy Trinity Guild. The aldermen of the guild were elected for life by all the burgesses and were obliged to name four burgesses every year who chose eight more. The twelve then elected the mayor and town officers.

NOTES

*Anything more like Bodmin Riding than the Ipswich Guild Procession we would, surely, be hard pressed to find. For, apart from the fact that the Ipswich Procession was not mounted, they seem almost identical in format and detail: the treasuries of both towns allow expenditure for their festivals; both have church connections and are whole town events; two guild officials in each town are responsible for the refreshments; the borough court in Ipswich and the guild court in Bodmin issue orders concerning the festivals and both have music; and, while trade companies march with banners in Ipswich, trade groups ride with garlands in Bodmin.
*The note on Lynn's guild illustrates how it gradually merged with the borough corporation itself; in fact, the Ipswich guild appears to have become closer to the municipal body than Bodmin's guilds had in the fourteenth century. Nevertheless, examples of guild activity in such places as Helston, Ipswich and Lynn may illustrate the ways in which Bodmin's developed and the Riding originated.
*We know that Bodmin had a Merchant Guild which had, by the fifteenth century, split into over forty trade and religious guilds. It is

evident: that some of the guilds, if not all, were connected with an annual town festival; that the mayor signed an ordinance connected with its observance; and that borough money was expended during the event.

We are sure, also, that when guilds disappeared from the town - presumably merging with the body politic which still meets in the Guildhall - the borough continued to maintain the festival until fairly recently. As the Ipswich Procession finally degenerated into a Corporation Dinner, so apparently did Bodmin's Riding, for, on page 35 of the October 1927 'Old Cornwall' journal, W.J.P. Burton's 'History Of Bodmin' is quoted in which he wrote that *the (Riding) day ended with sports, and a substantial dinner for the mayor and corporation*.

APPENDIX EIGHT

BRETON PARDONS & A 'RIDING'

THE TROMENIE

1) **G.H. Doble, 'The Saints Of Cornwall', part 4, page 94 (Truro Chapter, 1965)** showed that land granted by a local chieftain to a Celtic mission, which eventually became the property of a church or monastery, was probably what was meant by the word *minihy* in the Cornish and Breton languages. He drew attention to Locronan's procession called a *tromenie* held *"to preserve the memory of the exact boundaries of the minihy or monachia"*.

2) **Henry Myhill, 'Brittany', page 135 (Faber, 1969)** describes the Petite Tromenie held on the second Sunday in July at Locronan (south western Brittany) whose name means 'holy place of Ronan'. The 5th/6th century Celtic missionary evangelised the area and was buried there. One year in seven, a more elaborate festival called a Grande Tromenie occupies a whole week and villagers of the district *"make a circuit of the parish boundaries"*.

3) **Mary Elsy, 'Brittany & Normandy', page 82 (Batsford, 1974)** describes this circuit of the sanctuary or tromenie as *"rewalking St. Ronan's everyday barefoot route"*.

A 'RIDING'

4) **Miss Elsy, on page 101 of her book,** mentions that the place called le Tour-du-Parc in southern Brittany derives its name from the fact that *"noblemen who lived at Suscinio (chateau) near by used to make a tour round this area on horseback"*.

NOTES

*The tromenie is a particular kind of Breton parish feast which in general is known as a *pardon*. Usual activities on this annual occasion include a mass; an open-air service; a procession of priests and villagers carrying candles, banners and a shrine of the saint in whose honour they parade; and a fair with dancing to bagpipe music and wrestling.

*The procession, in the case of the *tromenie,* perambulates a boundary. The word derives from the Cornish and Breton *tro minihy* meaning *'circuit of the sanctuary'.* The definition of a *minihy,* as suspected in the first passage above, could well apply to Bodmin for the biography of Petroc depicts his dealing with several local chieftains. And, in fact, Charles Henderson considered that *"Bod-minihy (the house of the sanctuary)"* was *"a meaning far more in accordance with the oldest spellings"* of Bodmin *(Bodmine or Bodminia)* than the alternative 'house of monks' interpretation ('Cornish Church Guide', 1925; new ed. Barton, 1964)

*The third passage above is of utmost fascination. Miss Elsy's description not only corroborates what is known of the rigorous routines of Celtic 'saints' but, if gleaned from local sources fairly recently, also shows that Bretons still observe a tradition begun some fourteen hundred years ago. And moreover, unlike the Riding participants, they actually *know* they do!

*The fourth passage above includes a description of yet another example of bounds' beating on horseback. This was presumably to retain the castle's right to the land.

*To sum up - Brittany has much to teach us about Cornish customs. The necessity of knowing and of claiming exact boundaries was obviously important before titles to land were registered; and perambulations of them, either by walking or riding, were undertaken at least annually. The circuit of a sanctuary had a meaning beyond the normal parish and borough bounds' beating, however, in that extremities of land which had been sanctified by the evangelism of a Celtic saint were followed in his honour. If Bodmin was a *minihy,* then its Riding - already suspected as having had associations with bounds' beating and parish feasts - could have been a *tromenie:* a mounted *circuit of the sanctuary* of Petroc, possibly on the feast of a royal patron of his monastery, King Edgar. Until the Reformation in the 16th century, Bodmin town belonged to Petroc's priory; when it became a free borough, the beating of the town bounds could have parted company with the original tromenie so that, by the time descriptions of the borough-bounds'-beating and of the Riding enter the records, they were separate events.

PAT MUNN

The Story of Cornwall's Bodmin Moor (50p)

'an incredible attention to detail . . one must indeed applaud the amount of research put into the writing. .' Cornish Nation

'the best book . . which deals with . . the moor . . well worth its price . .' New Cornwall

'a work of meticulous research . .' B.B.C.

Introducing Bodmin, The Cornish Capital (70p)

'countless hours of research must have gone into collating this wealth of detailed information . .' Cornish Guardian

'a work of some scholarship . .' B.B.C.

'will appeal to anyone . . to see just how much lies behind (Bodmin's) deceptive facade . .' Western Morning News

L.E. LONG
An Old Cornish Town (£1)

Essays and anecdotes on bygone Bodmin, to be published in July 1975 including a centre-page-spread plan of the old county gaol and six pages of photographs, this volume is the first by the curator of Bodmin's museum. Essay subjects include the gaol, the Finn V.C. diary, inns, schools, mayors, leather and wool workers, the Basset funeral, and a study of parish field names.

EILEEN JONES
A Cornish Sanctuary

The story of a Londoner who discovered a gift for healing and settled in a Cornish village to practise it.
Expected late 1976.

Obtainable from booksellers; or, add 15%, direct from Bodmin Books Ltd., 45 Fore Street, Bodmin, Cornwall, PL31 2JA.